T0288283

THE
WORLD
THROUGH THE
DIME STORE DOOR

THE
WORLD
THROUGH THE
DIME STORE DOOR

———— *A Memoir* ————

Aileen Kilgore Henderson

The University of Alabama Press   Tuscaloosa

The University of Alabama Press
Tuscaloosa, Alabama 35487-0380
uapress.ua.edu

"In the Shadow of the Longleaf Pines" originally appeared in *New Letters* 77, no. 1 (Fall 2010–2011), published by University of Missouri–Kansas City.

Typeface: Scala Pro

Cover images: *(top)* S. H. Kress Co. five-and-dime store in Greensboro, North Carolina, photograph by Carol M. Highsmith, from Carol M. Highsmith's America Project, Carol M. Highsmith Archive, Library of Congress, Prints and Photographs Division; *(bottom)* The Kress 5, 10, and 25c Store, Hot Springs, Ark., postcard, courtesy of Phillip Pessar, CC BY 2.0
Cover design: Mary-Frances Burt / Burt&Burt

Cataloging-in-Publication data is available from the Library of Congress.
ISBN: 978-0-8173-2077-5
E-ISBN: 978-0-8173-9330-4

To Patrick and Anne Weston

CONTENTS

A NOTE TO READERS

WHEN A LOST AIRPLANE LANDED in our field in 1929, another world was opened to me. The two aviators stayed with us several days until Daddy could get enough money to buy the gas they needed to continue their journey. Immediately after they left, I wrote down on scraps of paper the details of their visit, the words that had been said and how they were said, reliving every minute of it. We didn't have a radio, I had never been to a movie, I had no books to read, and our Tin Lizzie had to be conserved for job hunting and other emergencies; therefore we could travel only as far as our feet would carry us. It was then I realized that writing was a way to hold on to the magic of life, to keep wonderful events forever. At age nine, I decided I had to become a writer.

Telling no one of my presumptuous decision, I began keeping a diary on any scrap of paper I could find. Later when Daddy worked with the Works Progress Administration at the University of Alabama typing the pages of Dr. Eugene Allen Smith's geology journal, he brought home to us discarded pages that were particularly interesting. I continued my accounts of our days on the backs of these used sheets. Later, Daddy gave me cast-off notebooks from places where he worked, and I kept on with my diary as well as drawing pictures to illustrate what I wrote. My English teacher in high school, Sarah Faucett, encouraged me to become a writer, and my English teacher at Judson College, Dr. Elsie Lewis, gave me even more encouragement.

But as an adult, earning a living took priority over writing. I relocated many times, and with each move, I took along the old boxes containing my diary even though the value of those scraps of paper had faded with the passing of years. I did manage to type most of the diary from the fading penciled scraps, but not until I was old myself did I find time to read the disorderly collection with attention. I intended to discard those pages that were dull and save only those worth keeping. But as I read, I became fascinated with the vivid past and decided to keep them all. This book evolved from those scribbled notes augmented with my memories.

The airplane that made Aileen decide to become a writer.

THE
WORLD
THROUGH THE
DIME STORE DOOR

The Kilgore sisters and cousins at Cedar Cove: (left to right) Cousin Junior and dog Tippy, Aileen, Mary Alice, Cousin Mary Lee, Francys, and Jane.

PROLOGUE

In the Shadow of the Longleaf Pines

IN 1921 I WAS BORN into Paradise, and nothing and nobody warned me that it wouldn't last. Seven years later, my parents hauled me away from Cedar Cove, clutching my cat Boodum in the back seat of our Model T Ford, and I never stopped looking back. Even when the mining camp itself was torn away and disappeared, I still refused to let it go. I can visualize each family living along the sandy road, beginning with ours—Mama, Daddy, Francys, Jane, Mary Alice, and me.

At our house, owned by the mining company, we ate in the dining room at a round oak table covered with a smoothly ironed cloth embroidered by Mama and spread over a silence cloth. Any day the menu might include steak, biscuits, Jell-O with whipped cream from the cows Mama kept, vegetables from the garden she grew, or chicken and eggs from her flock. And always cakes. Mama's cakes looked like the pictures in the magazines she subscribed to.

Yet I never missed a chance to eat butter beans with Crane and Emma Bigham and their six children (all of them larger than their parents) who lived across the road from us. I had a standing invitation to crowd my chair in at their kitchen table, spread with an oilcloth and set with gray enamel plates, battered forks, a large platter of cornbread, and a steaming pot of plump butter beans with ketchup and onions on the side. Eating was serious business, interrupted only to express a need—"Thank you for the salt," "Thank you for the cornbread"—and no one left the table until after Mr. Bigham had his coffee. Mrs. Bigham would pour the coffee from a gray enamel pot into Mr. Bigham's thick white cup. With a steady hand, he would turn a splash of the hot liquid into a thick white saucer, blow gustily across it, then siphon long swigs through his sand-colored mustache. Watching this ceremonial end to the meal contented me even more than the sameness of the menu—I thought nothing would ever change.

Boodum and I often sat on our front steps eating soda crackers— one bite for Boodum, one bite for me—watching for small muscular Mr. Bigham to stride out of his front door followed by his hefty sons, Anderson, Clarence, and Duke, all carrying their dinner pails and wearing their carbide head lamps. Garner, not quite of an age to follow his brothers into the mine, was usually involved in a building project with his friend Earl. Edna, nearing high school graduation, liked to rock on the front porch singing sad songs about pretty Red Wing, while Sara made the floorboards crack by dancing the Charleston and the Black Bottom. The Bighams sometimes held all-night dances that overflowed onto the porch, much to the delight of my spying eyes. Mr. Bigham did the fiddling; his friends furnished the jugs that passed from hand to hand in the shadows beyond reach of the porch lamp.

Up the hill from us Kilgores and Bighams lived the other mine employees, one house deep on each side of the road. Skipping past the Griffins, I would glance hopefully at the windows for a face admiring my nimbleness—perhaps tall, black-headed Ivey, or one of the twins, red-headed Ursra or black-haired Audry, or Bernis, a quiff of red hair topping his round, freckled face. Mr. and Mrs. Griffin looked so small and old that I wondered how they could have produced such a houseful of colorful children.

Beyond the Griffins lived Bonnie Wooley and her family. Bonnie invited Francys and Jane to parties at her house. Part of the entertainment was cooking dark-brown molasses candy, flinging the hot mass onto forked branches nailed to the wall, and pulling it into long strings over and over until it cooled into a creamy rope so brittle it could be broken into short lengths for everyone to share.

Farther on, the Mandersons' daughter and Jacob Snyder sometimes sat in the porch swing courting. For a few minutes, I'd loiter with the scruffy gang of boys toeing the edge of the Manderson yard singsonging, "Jacob Snyder, billy goat rider, he's a spider, he won't bite 'er."

Next came a place of magic, the schoolhouse. Inside were books with stories that I raced through, savored, and puzzled over. Here were teachers from town, attractively dressed (most Cedar Cove women wore ankle-length dresses aged into shades of gray under generous aprons), their faces softened with makeup (few Cedar Cove women wore makeup), women who traveled and told us things about the world. The schoolhouse drew everybody at one time or another for Valentine festivals, celebrations for Lincoln and Washington, church services (we'd raised the roof singing "Beulah Land"), box suppers, pie suppers, cakewalks, and dinners served by the Woman's Missionary Union (25 cents a plate).

Past Uncle Charley and Aunt Bessie's house, there was Grandmother's. She lived in what was called New Camp on the level top of the hill that once had been a plantation graveyard. All the monuments were buried in the graves or shoved off into the woods except two beside Grandmother's house. At night after Grandmother put me to bed, I would creep from under the net—what we called a "mosquito bar"— to stare out the window at the forgotten tombstones engraved with the name "Rush," wondering if their ghosts might be drifting among the houses and peeking in the windows.

Mama limited my stays with Grandmother to one week, and I went as often as she'd let me. Some of the time I played with my cousins across the road, James Hunter and Sissy Cox, and their collie, Tippy, but mostly I spent time with Grandmother, whom I loved. She allowed me to have coffee diluted with cream, served in a small china cup painted with roses and standing on four legs in a matching saucer. I didn't venture beyond Grandmother's, but I knew that where the houses dwindled out the miners had made a baseball diamond in an open field. Sometimes Daddy drove us in the Model T to watch Uncle Charley play on the miners' team.

Few if any of the mining families ever saw the homes of the company executives, secluded at the end of a long shady driveway. My sisters and I saw them because Mama had to take us with her on her rounds selling from the Larkin catalog. We played in the yard, while

Mama was invited inside the houses with their fancy entrances, no front porches, and no privies out back—but we wouldn't have traded our house for any of them.

The mine owner, Mr. Leake, didn't live in the camp. He and his son, Armistead, appeared periodically from somewhere smoking cigars and looking citified in their suits, ties, overcoats, hats, and shiny shoes. We coal camp children were proud that our fathers worked for them. Daddy, timekeeper and paymaster in the mine office, sometimes brought the Leakes to noon dinner at our house.

On miners' row, our houses were all alike, unpainted with a front porch, a back porch holding a shelf with a hydrant (the only water source), and five rooms in between heated with two fireplaces. Mama's garden took up most of our backyard. The clothesline was strung the length of it, and to the back stood the shed for our gentle cows, Mary and Martha. Behind that was the chicken house, the pigpen, and at the very back, the privy. Outside the fence, a forest of huge longleaf pines stretched down to the company doctor's house.

On our front porch Mama grew flowers in large glazed jardinieres. She lured into our yard fireflies, moths as big as hummingbirds, and butterflies to hover over her nasturtiums, zinnias, sweet-scented magic lilies from her childhood home in Pickens County, and climbing pink roses. Once when an elderly neighbor died, the women gathered on our porch to clip roses and sew them onto thick newspapers to make a fragrant canopy for his coffin.

Children of all ages turned the road into a playground with our mothers' approval—they did their work inside while keeping an eye on us, knowing there was no risk of a car coming. In the fierceness of shooting marbles for keeps (which was forbidden), the boys would forget their Sunday school lessons and blister each other with curses. When their tempers flared into a fight, they landed as many blows as possible before a mother could hurry outside, while we noncombatants chanted encouragement: "Fight! Fight! Ain't no kin. Kill each other. Ain't no sin." The boys also liked to show off the carbide they stole from their fathers' mining lamps, spitting their throats dry to make dabs of it sizzle and burn a hole in any skin it touched. Kick-the-can and hide-and-seek ranked high in our games because they accommodated few or many children, but baseball often ended in disappointment when Earl got mad and took the only bat, ball, and glove home. Lonnie and Stancil would stretch the huge snakes they killed in their chicken house full length in the road for us to nervously poke and pry and squeeze.

We'd thrill to danger that we fabricated. Forecasting our future with the fortune teller out of our Cracker Jacks—a piece of celluloid that reacted in our warm hands to predict riches and adventures. We added an omen to the list that came in the box: if the fortune teller rolled out of our hands, death had marked us. We kept our distance from the cracks that split the bare ground in dry weather—the devil's long hairy arm might reach out and grab us. Unless the sun shone through rain showers, then we knew he was busy beating his wife with a frying pan behind the kitchen door. When a thousand-leg crossed our path, we watched it with clenched jaws, knowing that worm needed only one glimpse of our teeth to make them rot in our heads. A ringing in our ears meant someone we knew had died—we'd look toward the tipple rising above the slate dumps, wondering if the mine tunnel had collapsed.

From the playhouses we made among the longleaf pines behind our house, we'd slip off to the doctor's to spy on his son Harry who'd then force us back with a barrage of rocks from the pile he kept ready. In the creek behind the Bighams' house, we built dams to trap minnows and tadpoles. Deeper in the woods, we wondered about the dipping vat, a long, deep groove dug into the ground looking like a cement-lined grave. Come summer, we'd hear the bellowing of the cattle as they were driven into the vat filled with a disinfectant solution to rid them of ticks and other pests.

Garner Bigham's flying jenny gave us our biggest thrill. On a sizable tree stump about three feet high, he loosely bolted a seesaw plank so that it revolved. One child would sit on either end while Garner pushed the jenny round and round, building momentum, going faster and faster until he had to duck away and let us "fly" by ourselves. We'd hold tight to the handle bar, dizzy and shrieking. Cousin Junior got so carried away he once wet his overalls.

Every weekday, Daddy walked down the wooded hill to the mining complex, which was made up of the commissary, doctor's office, post office, ice house, and other buildings required to run the Big Sandy Coal and Iron Company. Each payday, with a loaded pistol tucked beside the driver's seat, he drove to Dudley to meet the train and pick up the payroll money. As the men finished their shift, they lined up at Daddy's office to collect their earnings. Daddy called each one, Black and white alike, by name with a personal greeting remembered by many of them long after Cedar Cove died.

My sisters and I spent our mornings playing. In the afternoons, Mama helped us bathe, and we napped on a pallet until it was time to dress for Daddy's homecoming. He brought the mail and the newspaper. I'd lie on my stomach to read the funnies spread on the porch floor. *Boots and Her Buddies* was my favorite. Boots bobbed her blonde hair, wore trousers when she chose, flew her own plane, drove her roadster, and played the piano—things I had never seen a woman do.

My pretty sisters always made people glad to be with them. They went to birthday parties where they played games and were served "salitt on lettuce and . . . candy and ice cream with cherries . . . and cakes to," according to nine-year-old Francys's diary. They acted in school dramas and were invited to their friends' houses to play. In family pictures they are smiling—two of them had dimples—and looking like china dolls in their lace-trimmed dresses, as a cousin remembered long afterward. I was usually pictured squalling or sulking or wearing a torn dress with a bloomer leg hanging down below the hem.

From my beginning I loved cats. One day I played on the back porch with a litter of kittens I had confined in a galvanized tin washtub. I was teaching them to do tricks, but one kept rebelling and trying to run away. Losing patience, I seized him by the hind legs and beat his head against the side of the tub with all my might. By the time Mama got to me the kitten was dead. Not only did she whip me with a peach tree switch, but I had to sit in the back seat of the Model T with my solemn and sinless sisters while Mama drove us out in the country for me to lay the kitten's soft body among the wild ferns in the corner of a zigzag rail fence. My tears did not bring him back.

During one of Great-uncle Pat's visits, lost in my own world of play, I passed a few feet from his chair without noticing him. He caught

Aileen, bloomers flashing, jumps into her city cousin Mary Lee's specially posed photo. Sister Francys and Cousin Junior are behind her.

me around the neck with the crook of his walking stick and pulled me close. Holding me still with both hands, he studied my face. Then he released me with the loud verdict: "Ugliest child I ever saw in my life." His pronouncement did not mean much to me at that time. I was too content with my life as it was.

At the end of one of dainty Cousin Mary Lee's visits, her mother, Aunt Martha, dressed her in a new outfit: a red-plaid skirt, white blouse, a well-cut red jacket, and black patent-leather slippers. The adults gathered round her in admiration, and Daddy got out his Kodak camera to make a postcard-size picture of her to send to their friends back home in Pittsburgh. The rest of us cousins, sweaty and dirty from play, were instructed to keep our distance and absolutely not do anything to ruin Mary Lee's picture.

Socially poised Mary Lee gazed into the camera; Daddy snapped the shutter. Simultaneously, I leapt behind Mary Lee with bloomer leg dangling, Cousin Junior in overalls leapt behind me, and Francys behind Junior, all three of us smirking as if the picture were for us only. We did a thorough job of ruining Mary Lee's portrait, never realizing that when her parents showed the picture up north, they would have to explain their Alabama relatives.

Though I was impulsive and hot-tempered, I wasn't the one who nearly killed Francys on a beautiful summer morning. Great-aunt Mittie, while sweeping the front porch, dislodged a large jardiniere heavy with dirt and flowers. It fell several feet and landed on Francys as she came from under the house where we were playing. Aunt Mittie took one look at the broken jardiniere and smashed flowers, at Francys lying limp on the ground with a bleeding head, at the rest of us horror-struck children, and threw down the broom and screamed, "I've killed Francys!" She gathered up her long skirts and sprinted down the hill to the doctor's office, hollering all the way. Francys survived, and for the rest of her growing-up years, it was her head that caught most of the damage, in play and in sports.

At home, Mama fed us wisely, forbade us to walk barefoot near anybody's privy for fear of hookworms, made us wash our hands before we ate and our feet at night before going to bed, covered our beds with mosquito bars when we slept to ward off malaria, and periodically gathered us in the dining room to hand out biscuits, each with a bitter pink pill pushed into its soft heart, to keep us regular.

Our parents gave each of us a Bible, and I was not surprised to find my mother in the last chapter of Proverbs. Already I had decided that Mama's song was the hymn we sang in church called "Work for the Night Is Coming." She was busy from before daylight till after dark, cooking three meals a day, caring for her garden, and processing the food for our meals and for canning. She milked the cows and churned the clabber into butter and buttermilk. She washed and ironed for our family of six, and she sewed on her treadle machine far into the night making dresses. A dress Mama made from pale pink crepe de chine

Aileen's mother, Gertrude Cox Kilgore, and sister Francys, ca. 1918.
(The University of Alabama Libraries Special Collections)

with smocking across the yoke fed my vanity, as did one she made of white organdy with ruffles and a ruffled bonnet to match. When I wore them, I knew Great-uncle Pat had lied.

Mama helped with school events and took part in church, the Woman's Missionary Union, and prayer meetings. She walked over the camp selling products from the Larkin catalog, furnishing our house with some of the premiums she earned. When she had a moment to sit down, she tatted lace or embroidered napkins while I hung over her chair arm, watching—how she made French knots fascinated me.

Daddy was less serious about life, more playful. When we wanted syrup on our buttered bread, he didn't just pour syrup on the plate; he used the stream of condensed sorghum juice to make a farmhouse, a barn enclosed with a fence, farm animals, and fields with crops growing. He recited rhymes that made us laugh:

Going down the river, saw an alligator, turned my boat around, and shot 'im with a tater.

Possum up the simmon tree, raccoon on the ground, raccoon say to possum, "Shake them simmons down."

Amen, Brother Ben. Shot a rooster and killed a hen.

Beelah Bill, goin' uphill, kickin' up dust like an automobill.

At night in the light from the Aladdin lamp, Daddy cast shadow pictures on the wall with his hands—a barking dog, a rabbit, birds that flew, an alligator with teeth. Some days, every time he told us to do something, we'd say "What fer?" until finally he'd say "Cat fur to make kitten britches," which turned over our tickle boxes. While Daddy sharpened our pencils, I watched each precise stroke of his sharp-whetted pocketknife as it released cedar fragrance mingled with graphite and brought the pencil to a perfect point. One day I held Boodum while Daddy tied newspaper boots on his paws. The trick delighted me until I let Boodum go. He walked off stiff legged, lifting his feet high and shaking them and meowing complaints. "Take them off, Daddy!" I wailed. He did, but Boodum hid from me the rest of the day.

Our parents opened a bank account for each of us in the big bank in Tuscaloosa. We felt rich when Daddy showed us our little bankbooks and went over our deposits of nickels and dimes. He once drove us to see a black walnut tree that was so special—tall and straight with limbs and leaves only at the top—that somebody had paid a fortune to buy it. Another time he took us to Blue Pond, a water-filled crater on top of a hill. Everybody said Blue Pond was bottomless. Two boys had drowned there the week before, and men were dredging for their bodies while a crowd stood watching on the banks.

Christmas brightened our winters with gifts our parents chose with care. One year there were woven sewing baskets for Francys and Jane, china Bye-Lo baby dolls for all of us, and a folding blackboard and desk with chalk and erasers to play school. I once besieged Santa with prayers for a compact containing mirror, rouge, and lipstick, stressing the rouge and lipstick. When Santa delivered a pretty compact with only powder, I sulked the whole day.

Every Fourth of July we picnicked with Uncle Charley's family at the headwaters of Big Sandy Creek where the water roiled out of twin springs so clear and cold that within two minutes our teeth would begin clacking and our bodies turn blue. On the night of the Fourth, Daddy always supervised fireworks in our backyard—firecrackers, dazzling sparklers we held until there was nothing left but a red-hot wire, and Roman candles that went off with a boom and arced high in the night sky while we chanted, "I asked my ma for fifteen cents to see the elephant jump the fence. He jumped so high he reached the sky and never came back till the Fourth of July."

Late one April night in 1926, I was sleeping on a small bed in my parents' room when I heard Uncle Charley rapping on the window by my parents' bed and saying, "Sis, Mama's dying." He had been called out of the mine, and he now continued up the hill while my mother dressed to follow him. The next day, I went with Mama to Grandmother's house to oversee strange men working with bottles and instruments and tubes embalming her.

Some weeks after the funeral, my mother grieved herself into a nervous breakdown, ending up in Druid City Hospital in Tuscaloosa. That July Fourth my sisters joined Uncle Charley's family for the usual picnic at Big Sandy Creek, but I went with Daddy in our Model T to visit Mama. She talked a lot and cried and cried, and I couldn't understand why. I felt sad but not hopeless because I knew my daddy could fix everything. We stayed with her till dark. On the eighteen-mile ride home through the cool night, sitting beside Daddy on the front seat with the car top down, I believed our lives would become secure and happy again. Daddy made me laugh by swooping down the side of one hill and racing up another to send my stomach plunging into my feet. I didn't envy my sisters the fun they had with our cousins, James Hunter Cox and his sister, Sissy, playing in the cold creek and eating homemade lemon ice cream at Big Sandy.

Mama did not recover for a long time, not until she had two visions. One came at night; she awakened to see glowing lights, a large one and a small one, resting on the foot of the bed. The second vision came to her in the garden. Ahead on the row she was hoeing, she saw Grandmother in her long dress and bonnet, standing still, looking at her. No words were spoken but a feeling of peace came over Mama and the assurance that all was well with her mother.

When Gypsies caravanned into the valley and set up their carnival, our family went to the gala one-night stand. At a booth with a short artificial stream set into a tabletop, I netted a metal fish that opened like a pocketknife. Inside was a slip of paper that instructed the Gypsy to give me a small pan with a straight handle for cooking. It was made of aluminum, a wonder we'd heard about but had never seen. During the many years Mama used my prize, it was always called "Aileen's boiler," a lasting souvenir of happier times.

Not long afterward, we made our exodus from Cedar Cove. Even though Daddy had lost his job at the mine, we didn't realize that we were entering the Great Depression and an entirely new way of life. The years of the 1930s extinguished my daddy's spirit and taught me he couldn't fix everything. Those years took away our Model T, our bank accounts, our tablecloths and steak dinners. They canceled Santa Claus's visits, turned us into farmhands, and brought us a baby brother. Uncle Charley, a star of the coal miners' baseball team, eventually took his family to Detroit where he worked in an automobile plant. The older Bigham sons went to the coal fields of Illinois and Kentucky in search of work; the rest of the Bigham family relocated to another mining camp where Garner was terribly burned in an underground explosion. Cedar Cove lingered in our thoughts and in our conversations, our lost Paradise.

Not until I was middle-aged and my father was old did I learn the truth about Cedar Cove. I had already come to realize that the all-powerful coal company controlled every facet of our lives back then, but I never suspected that the owners consistently cheated the miners. As timekeeper, Daddy was required to record the tonnage dug according to the coal company, and it was from this record that the men were paid. But Daddy also kept a private record in a pocket-sized notebook where he wrote the company's tonnage and then noted the tonnage

(1928) Month.	Operating. Supplies.	Esti.Enventory. 1928.	Esti.Enventory. 1927.	Bal on Daily Charge.	Net Tons.
January.	$1,664.21	$8,701.44	$ ---	$ --- *6,7/7*	6,196
Febru'y.	1,564.16	9,439.16	7,307.74	--- *8,42?*	9,718
March.	1,925.82	9,317.67	7,020.64	1,900.40 *8,990*	9,781
April.	1,560.60	10,846.82	7,962.33	3,125.58 *8,453*	9,416
May.	2,474.43	9,883.73	8,358.20	2,668.56 *8,993*	9,496
June.	2,847.32	9,687.39	8,072.88	2,837.93 *8,2/?*	8,661
July.	1,437.45	9,684.40	8,224.25	2,472.28 *4,9/3*	5,241
August.	918.26	9,476.60		2,350.04 *4.2?7*	4,419
Septembr					
October					
Novembr					
Decembr					

On this paper Aileen's father kept a record of how the coal mine he worked for was cheating the miners. Under "Net Tons" is the true number of tons the miners dug each month. The handwritten numbers show how many tons the company credited the miners with digging, paying them accordingly (coal miners were paid by the ton).

actually dug by the miners. Daddy's assistant discovered what he was doing and reported him to the coal company.

I was playing nearby in the road the morning Armistead Leake came to talk with Daddy. I didn't understand why the two men stood out in the road instead of going in the house, or why they talked so seriously. Many years later, I learned that Daddy had been fired, and the Big Sandy Coal and Iron Company had sent Armistead Leake to demand the notebook. The coal company promised Daddy a month's salary while he looked for another job if he cooperated. If he refused, the company would make sure he'd never get another job in the coal fields.

Daddy knew that without a job he had no house for his family to live in and no income to feed and clothe them. He saw no way out except to keep his good reputation and hope to find work elsewhere. But before giving up the notebook, Daddy secretly removed the last page, the one for the year 1928. The page showed the number of tons the miners had *actually* dug each month, and beside that Daddy had written the number of tons the company had *paid* them for digging—a much lower amount. Since the miners were paid for the tons they dug, their pay should have been significantly more.

Daddy had put the notebook page in his dresser drawer where it stayed out of sight until he showed it to me in 1973. As I held the small paper in my hand, I remembered that Daddy hadn't found another job for a long time after we moved away from Cedar Cove.

"Did the coal company pay you the month's salary?" I asked.

"No," he said.

"Why didn't you threaten to expose them?"

He shook his head. "That would have been blackmail."

In reality there was no one to expose the coal company to. No union existed in the area to take up the miners' cause. The newspaper had no interest in a crusade. Jobs were too scarce in October 1928, and the future too dark, for anyone to complain against the mine owners.

But at the time, being seven years old, I knew nothing of this.

CHAPTER ONE

MOVING OUR HOUSEHOLD TO BROOKWOOD was a major undertaking. Our cows, pigs, and chickens, the plants and bulbs Mama wanted to keep, including the pink climbing roses and the magic lilies from where she grew up in Pickensville, all required special care. On the way to our new home, the open truck loaded with our household furnishings had to pull to the side of the dirt road when it came to the covered bridge over Big Hurricane Creek. The dresser, washstand, and bed Daddy had inherited from his parents were too tall to go through the bridge. The movers had to unload each piece, carry it through the bridge, then reload it on the other side. In irritation one of the men threw the marble top of the antique table from the truck to the ground, breaking it in half.

We settled into our precut Sears and Roebuck house set on twenty acres of waterless farmland. One word described the new house: grand. Light from the many large windows filled the spacious rooms, showing off the pretty wallpaper, chandeliers, and hardwood floors. French doors separated the dining room from the living room. The staircase entranced us—no mining camp house that we knew had a staircase. Ours led to a small room, mostly windows, perched on the roof. This "cockpit" marked our house as an Airplane Bungalow. More dazzling than any of this was the real bathroom—sink, toilet, and footed tub. A Delco-Light furnished electric power from a small outbuilding in which sat rows and rows of batteries. One of the batteries contained what looked like a mothball; when the ball neared the

The Sears premade mail-order house in Brookwood—the Kilgore family home starting in 1928.

bottom, the gasoline motor had to be run till the ball rose to the top again or the power would go out.

These wonders blinded us to two serious faults. The extensive brown stains that blotched the silvery paper covering the ceilings plainly announced a leaky roof, and the hot and cold water pipes threading the house had never felt a drop of water. During the following years, the sterile eighty-one-foot-deep well in the backyard gaped at us mockingly, symbolizing all the disasters that dogged us in our grand house on the hill.

Cheered on by our parents' hopes, we sisters, who had never had chores, set to work with willing hands. We collected the tin cans and rubbish that littered our acreage, all left behind by the former owners. We pulled up the burr grass—so painful to bare feet—that infested the field and burned it along with the trash we brought out of the double garage. Using the wheelbarrow, we cleared the fields of rocks, piling them against the fence, so Daddy could plow using a borrowed mule. We then searched the freshly plowed ground to gather the juicy Johnson grass roots for feeding our pigs. We toted water. Morning and evening my younger sister, Mary Alice, and I hiked to the Big Spring located about a mile down a wooded hill for our drinking and cooking water. Every night we made sure the woodbox behind the cook stove was filled and that there was a scuttle of coal for the living room fireplace. Francys and Jane alternated days of dishwashing. All four of us had to make beds and keep the floors cleared of newspapers, shoes, and debris.

Before long the newness of work and the team spirit broke down. We sisters quarreled, we complained, we stomped our feet in a temper, but usually ended up doing what we had to do. We realized that our poverty was connected with the rest of our country and extended to the whole world. In the magazines brought to us by Aunt Clara, we read stories about the stock market crash that made many men commit suicide because they had lost all their money. I was haunted by an article titled "Dragons Drive You." It was illustrated with a picture of a man clinging to a ledge outside a skyscraper window looking way, way down on a New York street ready to jump. We didn't understand that market crash but we knew it was disastrous for us all.

We realized the calamity of the Dust Bowl, too. At sunset we stood on the brow of our hill looking at the western sky. It was red, red, from one horizon to the other. "That's Oklahoma and Kansas blowing away," Daddy said. "They have no trees or grass left to hold down their soil."

Hitchhikers coming and going on the Birmingham–Tuscaloosa highway knocked on our door to ask for food or a place to sleep. Children we had never seen before came out of the woods to our back door with buckets asking Mama to sell them a nickel's worth of buttermilk.

A bright hope to me was the new consolidated school half a mile from home, but it was not finished in time to open in September. Impatient as I was, however, we were so busy that we were not ready until October either.

Shortly after our settling in, Mama was planting turnips in the garden when my cat Boodum made the first of his many trips back to Cedar Cove. He walked the twelve-mile round trip on his own unless our car had enough gas for my parents to fetch him or Uncle Charley brought him to me. The changes taking place at Cedar Cove must have finally convinced him it was no longer home. He settled down at our farm and lived to be an octogenarian in cat years.

We children still had our games, but they were different from our Cedar Cove games as we had no one outside the family to play with. Mary Alice and I imitated birds using our folded arms for wings to fly around the yard making bird sounds before perching on the woodpile or the homemade sawhorse. We collected dried cornstalks suitable for dueling—jabbing and parrying and scoring without drawing blood. I learned to cluck the different languages of the hens, and I became such an expert crower that on a hot summer afternoon I could awaken drowsing roosters for miles around to answer my challenge. We used the wooden spools Mama saved for us to dip in soapy water and blow bubbles. She showed us how to thread a button on a circle of string and then set the button in a blur of spinning by see-sawing the thread back and forth with our thumbs. Often Francys or Jane, in a big rocking chair on the front porch, sang songs out of Grandmother's hymnal.

My musical interest involved a Prince Albert harp. I asked Daddy to save me his Prince Albert tobacco can, then I hammered nail holes in the bottom, and put in different sized pebbles I had washed. I brought the top ends together, leaving a tiny slit to blow through to make the music. Whenever I found a Prince Albert tobacco can I saved it because I never knew when I might need another mouth harp.

For a time, Daddy worked at Fleetwood mine six miles west toward Tuscaloosa, driving in our topless car that icy, hungry winter. Mama heated bricks on the cook stove to help keep him warm. When that mine closed, Daddy bought from the company a very large cylindrical water tank to set on a platform he built. He shaped gutters out of old tin roofing and installed them to drain rainwater off the roof into the tank. We used rainwater for animals, bathing, shampooing, and washing clothes.

We supplemented the rainwater by filling cans, bottles, and buckets at the hydrant beside Mr. Martz's store across from the new school and loading them in the Model T. But the time came when we had to sell our Ford.

Mr. Martz at the store knew what a struggle we were having. One day Daddy came home with a big bag over his shoulder. In the heat of summer, worms had hatched in all the store's raisins and Mr. Martz gave them to Daddy. We sat around the bag in the living room picking worms out of each raisin: the worms to feed the chickens, the raisins for Mama to wash and feed to us.

We had no ice during those long, hot summers. Daddy built a sturdy box similar to a toolbox and fitted a lock to it. He set it in the ground to catch the overflow from the Big Spring; the water entered through an opening at one end to fill the box, keeping the submerged sweet milk, buttermilk, and butter cool, and flowed out the other end. At meal times Mary Alice and I went to the spring with the key and brought home whatever we needed.

Most of our clothes were cotton and had to be starched, especially in summer when everything wilted in the humid heat. Mama made our starch, mixing flour with water and cooking it with constant stirring to keep lumps from forming. For ironing, she had irons in three sizes— small, medium, and large. A fire in the cook stove kept them hot; two were always ready for use while she was ironing with the third.

In winter we shelled by hand the corn we had harvested. Daddy hauled it to the mill beyond Howton about three miles away in a two-wheel handcart he had made. Mr. McCoy ground the corn into meal with a gasoline engine, taking a measure of meal for his pay. Cornbread was a staff of life for us to accompany buttermilk and vegetables. If Daddy were sick or away looking for work, Mama wrapped Mary Alice and me in layers of sweaters and coats, and we two girls rolled off to the mill.

For a while Mama created chocolate milk from our cows' creamy milk, poured it into half-pint store-bought bottles that she had sterilized, covered each bottle with a store-bought cap, and carried the cumbersome load to the schoolhouse where she sold it for a nickel a bottle. She soon lost money though because children, looking famished, begged her to credit them "till tomorrow." She couldn't bear to think of them going hungry and let them have a bottle on credit. But the children forgot as soon as they drank her delicious mix and most of them never brought the money.

Alice Prude Smith, who lived halfway between our house and the school, also suspected how things were with us. Miss Alice had grown up on a prosperous farm near Tuscaloosa and was better off than we were. During our neediest Christmas, she invited Francys and Jane to spend the holiday with her. This gave my two older sisters some cheer, since in our home there was no money for even the simplest celebration. Mary Alice and I, without a stocking in the house, set a box top down at the fireplace on Christmas Eve night. We posted ourselves in a room with east-facing windows, knowing that Santa Claus would come from that direction, determined to catch him. Every hour or so Mama came in to encourage us to give up, but we stayed on staring out the window, watching, getting colder and colder. Finally we decided Mama was right—Santa wouldn't come as long as we watched for him—so we crept off to bed, oversleeping the next day. There were no exclamations of surprise or joy when we discovered our box tops held a Milky Way candy bar each and a few nuts and raisins. Another Christmas, Mama took from a cow-feed sack two doll patterns, which she cut out, sewed together and stuffed, adding some embroidery on the face and garments. We loved those dolls!

Miss Alice was married to Oscar Smith who owned a cotton gin. Mr. Oscar had worked as a chain gang guard at the convict camp above the Big Spring near our house, though the camp had been closed by the time we moved there. His job was to take the prisoners out to work the roads, guard them with a gun, see that they did the work, then get all of them back to camp at dark. But when the guards began whipping the prisoners at night he couldn't stand that and quit.

A Black neighbor of ours, Roy Morgan, also told about the camp. He said that night after night from his house he would hear the cracking of the whips and the men crying out and begging for mercy. "If there is a God in heaven, some of those guards are sure going to hell," he said.

Just before Christmas 1932, our brother was born during a winter when even the bathroom toilet froze and broke, and frozen pipes pulled the sink from the wall and laid it on the floor. My mother had no prenatal care. Not one word was said to us girls about what was happening, but I noticed changes in my mother's body and finally figured out she was pregnant. She had constant heartburn and sought relief by drinking baking soda water. I feared that drinking too much of that wasn't good for her. I pictured the soda washing over the baby, taking off its hair and skin, leaving a raw and bloody body. She continued doing the farm chores, with me always lurking around to help if she would let me.

One day the cow flung back her head, striking Mama in the stomach with a horn. A damaging bruise spread over her distended belly— I'd see it at night when she rubbed it with oil. I trembled to think the baby was dead or that Mama would die. Then she caught a severe cold. She sat up many nights so wracked with coughing that I thought her insides would surely come up. I longed to do something for her but didn't know what, and in her misery she said nothing, not even a complaint.

Unbeknownst to us, she wrote Cousin Mary Lee's mother in Pittsburgh asking for money for the doctor. When the next letter came from Aunt Martha, we gathered around Mama's rocker eager to hear news, as letters were rare. I noticed, as Mama read aloud, that she skipped part of the letter, but I glimpsed enough over her shoulder to know that Aunt Martha sent no money and scolded Mama and Daddy for having another baby. Mama quickly folded over that part of the page so we couldn't read it, and I never saw the letter again.

Daddy was home December 22, 1932, which was the last day of our school year—the county had no money to pay teachers for the spring semester. Before leaving earlier than usual for the half day of school, we stood around Mama's bed where she lay writhing and wringing the iron bars of the bedstead, her eyes glazed, not looking at us, her face twisted in anguish. Not a sound did she make and we said nothing. On the way to school, we did not talk of what was happening at home. My sisters' hearts must have been as cold and heavy as my own, but we did not comfort each other.

I have no memory of that school day until the dismissal bell. In the crowd on the way out, a classmate coming in the front door laughed at me and shouted, "Aileen has a new baby brother! Aileen's mother had a baby!" I was furious to hear the news proclaimed in such a light-hearted way, news that might mean my mother was dead. On Decoration Day at the Big Hurricane Cemetery, I had put flowers on the many graves of women who had died having babies. Usually the baby was buried with them. Some of my classmates were orphaned that way; they too brought flowers for their lost mothers.

Trudging the endless mile home that December day, I was eaten alive with fear and burning with the hurt that I had to hear about the baby in that way. I found my sisters standing around my mother's bed; other people were there and Daddy was in the background, smiling. I knew that he loved his girls but to finally have a boy with his name, William Oscar, was his great joy. The doctor from McCalla had left a box of horehound candy sticks for the four sisters, but I refused to take one. I crept to our bedroom where I found Francys standing in the center of the room, tears in her eyes. We didn't speak, and later people said we were jealous to have a baby in the family, but Francys, now fifteen, knew better than I did the price Mama paid for this baby and what meager funds we had to care for him.

Where Daddy got the money to pay the doctor the twenty-five dollars for "bringing our brother" I did not know. Our farm work brought in no cash money, and cash money we had to have not only to buy food but to pay for textbooks (always second- or third-hand), insurance, our mortgage, and other expenses. Sometimes Daddy could earn our school fees by doing some kind of work at the school.

Daddy wore out the soles of his shoes walking up and down the graveled highway that connected Tuscaloosa and Birmingham searching for work. The trip to Tuscaloosa was seventeen miles, and Birmingham was about fifty-five miles. He caught a ride when he could, but not many people had cars so rides were few. He became an expert at using the resoling kits sold by the dime store to renew his shoes.

He entertained us with stories of what he encountered along his route. The worst hurdle was a house in Jefferson County marked by an apple tree out by the road. A man-eating dog lived there and it especially hated Daddy. The dog seemed to know whenever he was coming, and it would lie in wait when he came in sight of the house.

With stiff hackles and a deafening roar it would shoot out of its hiding place like a cannon ball straight at Daddy, spitting saliva at every roar. "Wouldn't be so bad," Daddy told us, "if it kept the same hiding place. Then I'd know where to expect it. But it changes every time." And so Daddy steeled himself to walk on without any defensive or aggressive gestures. "Just to get past in one piece is all I want," he said. In the telling he never mentioned how tired and hungry he must have been as he contended with that obstacle. He laughed when he told us that he had an incantation he used when his feet lagged: "Pickin' 'em up and puttin' 'em down," he told himself at every step.

Later on, in desperation he borrowed money from Uncle Davis for a trip to Joe Wheeler Dam in North Alabama to offer himself as a laborer. On March 21, 1935, he wrote Mama:

Arrived here at the Dam 2:30 P.M. yesterday. Found Mr. Cannon (Davis's man) and did not get to talk to Mr. Ellis until 10 o'clock this Morn. They were full up on laborers and carpenter helpers but I kept talking to him and when I told him about my supply house equipment experience he got interested and gave me note to Mr. Roby, Master mechanic, to interview me as equipment clerk. I went down to see him at the Dam. He asked me a few questions and said he had some work to get off and asked me to come back about 1:30 P.M. Afraid to feel too good over it. Might get disappointed. I understand the job pays $105.00 per month, board here at Bunk house cost $29.50 month. So don't feel too good over it for it might not be true.

Hope you all are o.k. If I get to work will send dollar or two of the $5 Davis gave me.

This river sure is pretty here at Dam. It's one and a fourth mile wide here.

Tell Buddy [William] I'll send or bring him some gum.

Yours, Oscar

Daddy trudged home looking thin and gray. Days passed and no word came from the dam. About this time, Daddy said that maybe the reason life was going so hard for us was that we weren't thankful enough. We waited, seated at our round dinner table, while he said a most wonderful prayer of thanksgiving. Ever after that, when everybody was seated at the table we had the blessing before eating.

No matter how little we had to eat, Daddy always thanked Mama for preparing our food and told her how delicious it was. From this, I developed the habit of going around the table after I'd finished eating to hug and kiss Mama. At times love for my parents overflowed my heart. The wild shrub growing in our woods named hearts-a-bustin'-with-love had special meaning for me.

Finally Daddy, a skilled telegrapher, an accurate accountant, an exact timekeeper and paymaster, had to go to work with the Works Progress Administration, one of President Roosevelt's projects. Every morning at six with his sunhat and lunch, he caught the WPA work truck and spent the day working on the roads.

We read in the newspaper the jokes about the WPA workers, how they spent most of their time leaning on their shovels, how the WPA handshake was "You shake, I'm too tired." But we knew some of the men began their day hungry and might have only a baked sweet potato in their overall pocket for their lunch.

Fortunately for us, the government allowed a WPA worker to accept other work as long as the income didn't exceed a certain amount. By persistence after many trips to Birmingham, Daddy had gotten himself on the extra board of the Frisco Railroad as a telegrapher. His calls to work came through Pierce's store in East Brookwood, the nearest telephone to our house. Some of the boys hanging out at the store would leap on whatever mode of transportation they had available that day, usually an old truck somebody was working on, and drive the two miles to our house to let Daddy know. In return, he always gave them a "set-up" of a penny Baby Ruth, or chewing gum. The railroad calls took precedence over the WPA or any other work because he needed to build up his seniority. That was the way to a regular job.

Being on the extra board meant that he had to go wherever the railroad needed him, ranging from Arkansas to Florida, for one day or several. He had to study the railroad rulebook and learn what each job on the entire line required for first trick (7:00 A.M. to 3:00 P.M.), second trick (3:00 P.M. to 11:00 P.M.), and third trick (11:00 P.M. to 7:00 A.M.).

Daddy was away most every Christmas because men on the regular railroad payroll wanted off at that time. One year, from December 18 to January 10, he worked at Demopolis, Aliceville, Pratt City, Freight Yard Junction (in Birmingham), and Dora—all in Alabama—and Tupelo, Mississippi. He skimped on food and slept on a table in the depot or a cot if one was available. At one place he got so cold that he nearly froze to the bed, he wrote us.

My father had learned telegraphy from his uncle Bertic Morris, an agent at the railroad depot in Cottondale, Alabama, when he was fifteen years old. The night that lightning struck the great cotton mill Daddy could see the burning mill from the depot where he was working. He helped in the effort to save the loaded railroad cars in the mill yard waiting to be hauled away to market. "Send engines posthaste to pull the cars to safety," he told us was the message telegraphed to the Tuscaloosa railway yard. But the distance was too far and help too slow coming. The mill was never rebuilt and its employees, many already wheezing and coughing from brown lung disease, which was caused by breathing cotton dust, were without work.

After that, Daddy was hired by Alabama Great Southern Railroad and became third-trick operator at the AGS station in Tuscaloosa. When we had a car, he would sometimes drive us down Greensboro Avenue in Tuscaloosa, and Mama showed us the boardinghouse she lived in when they were courting. Back then, Daddy would stay with her till the last minute before sprinting down Greensboro to the depot for work. After they married, he left the railroad because Mama didn't like to be alone at night. He went to work with the mine at Cedar Cove as timekeeper and paymaster for $108 a month. By the time he lost that job, all the other local mines were closing and there was no position for him.

Though Mama had her hands full with putting food on the table, caring for the animals and the garden, and washing and ironing our clothes, she still tried to find ways to make money. One year she and Sid, who lived on the hill beyond the Big Spring, planted a cotton crop on shares. Sid had a mule, and Mama had herself and us girls to do the hoeing and picking. The partnership didn't gee-haw smoothly. Sid was a "come day, go day, and God send Sunday" farmer and Mama was for "doing it now while the weather holds." My dusty yellow cat with the cutest nose, Genevieve, followed me as I hoed, lying in the shade of the cotton plants to watch me. Ole Grandmaw Pig kept Francys and Jane company the same way.

When picking time came in October, each of us had a clean tow sack to shoulder. Picking wasn't easy or painless. Until then I had thought hoeing and picking velvet beans was the worst work, because the velvet from the black beans got all over us and set us on fire. But picking cotton was harder on the back and brought the blood out of our fingers with the sharp pricks. For our cotton picking though, the weather stayed clear and with Mama's help we finally finished.

Then we had to get the cotton to the gin in Northport. Mama hired a Mr. Brown who drove his rick-rackety topless Chevy truck into our yard one day with his gaunt red hound dog sitting beside him. He shoved the dog into one of our chicken coops and left him in the shade of the backyard. "I been down to Duncanville huntin' rabbits and coons," he explained.

Our next step was to tote the cotton out of the back bedroom where we'd stored it and pile it on the truck. It was then we realized the truck had other shortcomings besides being topless—weak sideboards that might not withstand the weight of our precious cotton, no windshield, no horn, no door, threadbare tires—we stopped looking and kept loading. The cotton towered higher than the driver's head and there was no seat for Sid. He had to lie on top of that precarious load. Mama sat on a wooden box beside Mr. Brown. We watched them rocking and bucking down the lane, Mr. Brown clenching tight to the steering wheel, Mama sitting on her purse and holding to the box with one hand and her hat with the other, Sid cringing down into the cotton with nothing to hold on to. At the gin they ended up with a bale weighing 510 pounds and compliments from the ginner: "That's the best cotton I've seen this year," he said. Mama and Sid sold their bale at the gin and divided the money. Then Mr. Brown brought them home, Mama paid him, he reclaimed his red hound, and we thought that was the end to the cotton story.

But it wasn't. Mary Alice and I were gleaning the leftover cotton (to be sold for two cents a pound) when Sid tore into the field demanding to know Mama's whereabouts. "She's cheated me!" he roared. "She owes me five dollars more!" He headed for the house. Mama was shocked to see him, but that night as she refigured their finances, she decided she did owe him two dollars more. If she had owed him five dollars more, she would not have cleared a thing out of that year of hard work.

Another one of her projects didn't work out either. A Mrs. Boone advertised for someone to take care of her blind and bedridden father for fifty dollars a month. She came by to look us over but we didn't hear from her again.

Mama took in boarders, teachers at the school, girls going to summer school at Brookwood High, men working for the strip mine companies. This more than doubled her workload and kept her constantly on the lookout for food possibilities.

She entered contests galore that appeared in magazines for furnishing the last line of a jingle or answering a puzzling question. Participation cost nothing except postage, which we had a hard time scraping up sometimes. From one of her efforts, she won a history book that had no pictures. Francys had priority on saving matchbox labels for free teaberry gum, and Jane won a miniature camera by saving labels. Buddy found a hubcap in the ditch by the road. He sold it for twenty-five cents to the insurance man who came to collect the weekly burial insurance premium.

When our cupboard was empty, Mama decided we could give up one of the metal drums we used to collect rainwater. Aunt Janie and her husband, Mr. Will, Black neighbors of ours, came with their oxcart and money to pay for the drum. Aunt Janie also brought a letter for Mama to read to them. It was from their daughter, Ida Mae, who had gone away to West Virginia and "fell in style," drinking and smoking, Aunt Janie lamented.

Whenever we had a pig killed, Mama sent word to Aunt Janie to come for some of it. Mr. Will would bring the oxcart and load up their portion. Mama would save the bladder to make a balloon for Buddy. She said all the Christmas they used to have growing up in Pickensville came from saving the bladders at hog-killing time and blowing them up and bursting them.

No matter how hard Mama and Daddy scrimped and pinched, the year came when the newspaper listed our farm among those up for sale for nonpayment of taxes. Mrs. Shook from Kellerman, who was interested in buying the house, came to inspect it. My sisters disappeared somewhere but I followed as Mama guided her through each room.

"I've loved this house since the first time I saw it," Mrs. Shook said. "It's beautiful, so light and airy, such large windows."

I watched and listened as Mama showed her through each room, wanting to hate her but I couldn't. Her comments were kind and thoughtful and not at all biggety.

But once again another of President Roosevelt's programs saved us. Before the sale could take effect, Daddy applied for a loan through the government-sponsored Home Owner's Loan Corporation, which not only paid our taxes but made some repairs on the house, including a new roof. We still had our mortgage payments to make and now the sixteen-dollars-a-month HOLC payments, but I no longer lay awake at night wondering where we'd live if we had to move.

During my elementary school years, Mama took us to the after-school programs that were provided for the community. Two very different ones were memorable to me. Miss Ray, daughter of our first principal, played classical piano compositions for us on her own grand piano that had been moved to the school's stage just for the day. I was not so much enthralled by the music as I was by her technique: when she crossed her wrists and continued playing, I thought she must have gotten mixed up. And I loved the tone of her piano and the beauty of its construction. In my eyes it was truly grand.

The other program was an informal talk by Brother Bryan, a famous preacher from Birmingham. I was impressed by his silver hair and saintly face and by what Mama said about him. As Mrs. Smith, seated beside Mama, bragged that Brother Bryan, on the coldest day, would take off his own coat and give it to a needy person, Black or white, Mama commented, "What a trial he must be to his wife!"

When I asked her later what she meant, she said, "He'll get chilled and come down with pneumonia. Who'll doctor him? Who'll sit up nights with him? What about all their children catching his germs—who has to take care of them? And his wife will have to find another cloak for him."

I embraced school and learning with my whole being and as a result was double promoted twice before I reached sixth grade. But that year produced some things that were too astonishing for even me to believe. In sixth grade, our history book stated that two thousand years ago the Romans had running water in their houses! I knew of only two of my classmates that fortunate: Virgie who lived across from the school and Lora who lived a few houses from her. Everybody else toted water from a spring, as Mary Alice and I did, or else had a well on the back porch or in their yard.

Roy, also a sixth grader, gave me another shock telling me that the stars didn't go out when morning came—they stayed shining steadily all the time. I wouldn't have it, but Roy helped his grandpa dig wells and he insisted, "You go down in a hundurd-foot-deep well even on the brightest day and you'll see, Miss Smarty. Them stars never do go out." Even after Miss Walker backed him up, I didn't believe him. I wanted the world to be my way.

The one world that I embraced without question was created by Great-aunt Mittie. In the coldest part of winter, when her tarpaper shack in Pickens County could no longer hold the wind at bay, and she had no firewood because her son Willie, a veteran of the 1918 war, was ailing (drunk), she came to our house. After supper every night, we sat close around the fireplace, Aunt Mittie in the middle, while she told magic tales. She embellished the stories with plot twists of her own and used old-time language from the Mississippi Delta of fifty years before, all of which I loved. One of our great favorites was "Beauty and the Beast"—how my heart grieved for the Beast dying alone under the Lady Banks rosebush. And the tale of the light-footed Cinderella with the certain happy ending was another satisfying story to go to bed on.

But "Bluebeard" was my favorite. What drama! It was like listening to a radio program or play with Aunt Mittie speaking all the parts:

THE KITCHEN CAT. Mistress, if you'll give me a saucer of cream, I'll lick that blood off the key for you.

THE YOUNG WIFE, *clutching the key to the Little Red Room in her hand and frantically searching for a way to remove the blood stain.* Out of my way, you no-count moggy! I'll kick you into the middle of next week! (*And she sends Kitty sprawling with a loud "Meow" of pain.*)

BLUEBEARD, *at the foot of the stairs, sharp sword in hand, roars.* Come down from up there! ["He had a game leg," Aunt Mittie explained. "That's why he couldn't go upstairs and fetch her."]

SISTER ANNIE, *on the upstairs balcony, straining her eyes to see in the distance.* Nobody in sight. Not a soul.

(*The sword rattles at the foot of the stairs.*)

BLUEBEARD *roars.* I'm gonna add you to the Little Red Room! (*And he stomps his feet.*)

THE YOUNG WIFE, *distraught and pacing the floor and wringing her hands.* Sister Annie! Don't you see anybody coming?

SISTER ANNIE. Only the cotton blossoms waving in the breeze.

THE YOUNG WIFE. Sister Annie, look hard! Isn't *anybody* coming?

SISTER ANNIE, *on the balcony shades her eyes.* I see a dust cloud. . . . It's bigger, bigggg. It's drawing nearer! Nearer! It's Brother on his white horse! (*Jumps up and down, screaming.*) Hurry, Brother! Whip that pony!

BLUEBEARD *roars.* Come down from up there! (*Starting up the stairs, groaning at every step.*) [Aunt Mittie groans.] You'll be number twenty-one! Prettiest of them all!

THE YOUNG WIFE. Wave your handkerchief, Sister Annie! Wave your handkerchief!

No matter how many times Aunt Mittie had told the story, my heart was in my mouth and I wanted to leap up and wave and holler too.

But winter always came to an end, and Aunt Mittie went back to Pickens County to see about Willie, leaving me with memories of her enchanted worlds, and her assurance that our family was of the Blood Royale, though she never clarified which royal line she meant.

———

Summers brought a bounty to the countryside that was ours for the picking. We scavenged for blackberries that Mama turned into jams (with the seeds, for those with good teeth) and jellies (with the seeds strained out). How delicious the purple sweetness was early mornings on our buttered and toasted cornbread. When the peaches ripened, she made preserves to go with the buttered biscuits that she'd make if we had flour. Two special peach trees grew on our fence row. One produced a clear-seed fruit, white inside and sweet; we ate these peaches just as they were. The other, a cling-seed peach with red meat, Mama used to make peach pickles. We peeled these peaches leaving them whole, and Mama pickled them, usually in pint jars. A shelf filled with jars of peach pickles was a mouth-watering sight.

As we roamed with our buckets and baskets searching for plunder, we sometimes came upon old home places marked by crooked, scaly apple trees that were still producing. With whoops of joy, we harvested apples with a grateful thought for the person who planted them. After washing the fruit, we'd cut the peeled apples into thin slices, then Mary Alice and I would climb to the tin roof of the two-room house where we stored fodder and other animal foods, stretch out clean sheets, and spread the slices to dry. The roof was too high for house flies to blow the fruit (lay eggs) and the sun above with the hot tin beneath dried the apples well. However, the danger was rain. Mama watched the sky, and if a threatening cloud rose up, Mary Alice and I had to speed to the roof, gather the sheets of apples, and speed down. (I didn't want lightning to catch me on that tin roof!) What tasty fried pies those apples made on a cold winter day.

Another way we children helped with the winter food supply was working at the community canning center that had been set up in a log house at the Big Spring. We shelled peas, peeled pears, snapped beans, scalded tomatoes, and did anything else in order to be allotted a share of the end product. That chair got so hard as we worked we thought we'd grow callouses on our setters!

We also roved the hills searching out plum thickets, eating our fill of the red and yellow fruit, and piling our buckets to bring home. And oh! Low-bush huckleberries and later on high-bush huckleberries, so loaded with fruit the bushes looked blue.

*Aileen in overalls with Francys (left) and Jane in front
of the pink "Dorothy Perkins" rosebush their mother had
brought from her old home in Pickensville.*

Our parents had to be weather forecasters as we had no other way
to know what was going to happen. However, a killer weather event
that nobody could predict was a tornado. We stood in our backyard
in March 1932 about four in the afternoon staring toward the north-
west sky where a black cloud seemed to stand still. We studied and
discussed, but couldn't fathom what it meant until we heard the next
day that Northport, across the river from Tuscaloosa, had been blown
away by a disaster out of the sky.

Otherwise, if an ordinary thunderstorm was likely to roll in, we
didn't want to get caught far from home, or if a freeze was on the way,
we wanted to save as much as we could from the garden. Mama and
Daddy studied the sky, the direction the clouds moved, or if they stood
still, tested where the wind was coming from, and noted what date it
thundered in February because on that date in April we'd have a frost.
And some people always planted beans on Good Friday.

If the signs indicated a freeze, we busied ourselves picking everything we could, whether it was ready or not. There were always many
green tomatoes on the vines. We pulled every one, wrapped them indi-
vidually in newspapers, and stored them in a big drawer in the kitchen

cabinet. Slowly they ripened and we had tomatoes for sandwiches and soups till after Christmas. Squash we wrapped and stored in the kitchen closet; cucumbers were hard to keep but I tried, for I enjoyed cuke sandwiches. Irish potatoes and carrots could stay in the ground safely with a blanket of pine straw; sweet potatoes we dug and stored under the house covered with a thick layer of pine straw.

A food supply for winter was all-important and school lunches had to be provided for. But whether I had a half sandwich or a syrup biscuit, my joy in school continued as I entered seventh grade still wearing my daily uniform: bib overalls and a shirt, no undergarments. Mama washed my outfit on the weekends while I stayed in bed in my nightshirt reading or drawing in my big book. Our teacher, Mrs. Wilson, had transferred to our new school from Muddy Branch School. We shared our room with the eighth grade, which was interesting because we could observe what occurred in both grades. Friday was the high point of each week for me because that was *Weekly Reader* day. I read every word and studied the pictures. The great world out yonder fascinated me.

During discussion time when Mrs. Wilson asked, "Who is the ruler of Manchuria?" nobody raised a hand except me. I was bursting to tell. The story came from one of my favorite parts of the world, the mysterious Far East. Mrs. Wilson waited for another hand. By now I was levitating. She *had* to call on me! When she did I almost shouted, "Henry Pooh Yigh!" Thunderous silence followed, then an explosion of laughter from both sides of the room that raised the roof. I looked around, not understanding. What was funny? Nobody could tell me— they were all laughing too hard. I flushed red, and redder still. I hid my hot face in my arms on my desk. I never again took part in the *Weekly Reader* discussions.

With Mrs. Wilson, for the first time we studied science. She conducted experiments on her desk while we watched from our desks. Then she dictated from a worn notebook what she had done and what the experiment proved. We laboriously copied her words into our notebooks. We used penny pencils and felt guilty if we wasted a sheet of paper.

When the weather was dark and dreary or we'd had a difficult day, Mrs. Wilson halted schoolwork and called on twin seventh graders Freda and Vesta to sing for us; "Silver Haired Daddy," "Maple on the Hill," and "Nobody's Darling" were favorites. After their song session everybody felt better.

CHAPTER TWO

MY JUNIOR AND SENIOR HIGH school years, from 1934 to 1938, brought about a great change in me personally. I stopped being the merry mischievous butterfly of our coal camp days, when the whole known world was my apple pie with sugar sprinkled on it, and became someone who knew that she was not likeable and, worse, that Uncle Pat had been right—ugly I was, freckled and snaggletoothed. Mama braided my long straight hair—called "dishwater blonde" by my Detroit cousins—and pinned the braids at the nape of my neck. The hand-me-down clothes I wore, too big for my skinny body, combined with my hairdo, eyeglasses, and prissy way of speaking correct grammar, made me personify Miss Minerva, the spinster in the William Green Hill books. Besides all that, one of my brown eyes was covered by a white scar that blinded it and made it look in a different direction from the other.

But the important thing for me was my attitude—I didn't let myself care. It was Mama who would not accept that I was not well-liked. She thought that pinning my limp hair up that way made me look neat, and that the A grades that labeled me a bookworm and got me exempt from final exams every year were something to be proud of. She spent a dime—ten whole cents that would have bought a loaf of bread or twenty oatmeal cookies—for an autograph book with pastel pages to pass around among my classmates for them to record their professions of friendship. I didn't let her see the result: nothing personal but page after page of rhymed comments.

Tie a mule to a tree, pull his tail and think of me.

I thought, I thought, I thought in vain. At last I thought I'd write my name.

Don't be discouraged though jobs are small and few. Just remember that the mighty oak was once a nut like you.

I refused to let the lack of friends cause me grief. There were too many things that interested me. First in importance after studying was reading books. The P. C. Wren books, about three British brothers who joined the French Foreign Legion after the disappearance of a valuable ring, were such favorites that I copied in longhand page after page in order to keep the story for my own after I returned the book to the school library.

Naturally, I chaired the library committee. That involved making sure there was a volunteer librarian for each period of the school day who would keep order, check out books to the students, and make certain the books on the shelves were in the correct place. In addition, I decorated three bulletin boards and filled them with jokes, pictures, interesting tidbits, and bits of poetry that fired my imagination like "There's a schooner in the offing, / with her topsails shot with fire, / and my heart has gone aboard her / For the Islands of Desire" and "Great grandad, when the land was young, / Barred his door with a wagon tongue." Whether or not anyone ever looked at my arrangements didn't matter; my joy was in offering them.

Playacting was another interest. I loved becoming someone else though it usually involved—of course—an old lady part. Mr. Gates, coach and geometry teacher, asked me to partner him in a comedy sketch between the acts of a school show. In the skit, I was a hard-to-get old lady and he was an old man courting me. We got accolades for that. Then I was chosen for the lead in our senior play, *Aunt Samantha Rules the Roost*. Another old lady part, but the laughter of the audience was music to me. Later, an elderly grandfather in the community told me, "I wasn't going to bother going to that play but Aunt Samantha made me glad I did. You've got that ole lady business down pat."

Old lady or not, I ranged the world through the essays I wrote (we called them themes). I was fascinated by General Gorgas, an army doctor from Alabama who helped control yellow fever, saving many thousands of lives and enabling the Panama Canal to be built. My story about him won a handsome medal from the Gorgas Memorial Institute, a coppery brass circle with a relief of General Gorgas's head suspended from a royal blue ribbon. The school principal called me into the office and handed the box containing the medal to me with the words "Oh, yes, Aileen. This came for you." At first, I longed for him to make a presentation in chapel, but then I realized how much of a scaredy-cat I would have been before the whole school, and I was content to accept it inconspicuously. The faculty's selection of me as Miss Citizenship was another honor that came to me quietly and with the same surprise.

None of my activities appealed to my classmates, but that was not my fatal flaw. What made me not quite human to them, my absolutely unforgiveable defect, was my total lack of interest in football. Afternoon classes were canceled when there was a game at our school, and students who couldn't afford the ten-cent admission stayed in the study hall. From there we could hear the cheers and songs, adapted from the University of Alabama. When we played MacAdory High School the chants would be "Barney Google, Andy Gump, we've got MacAdory up a stump" or "Watermelon, watermelon, watermelon rind, look on the scoreboard and see what you find: Brookwood, Brookwood, leading the line, MacAdory, MacAdory waaaaaaaayyyy behind!" MacAdory always beat us. My classmates yearned to be outside at the game, but I was content to spend that time reading, studying, or drawing pictures to illustrate my diary.

Capping my school career was an incident in the library. I was the librarian for that period. At a table sat the six most popular members of my class, looking at magazines, giggling, writing notes, and whispering. I had no idea I was their subject until one of the girls walked past me where I sat in the librarian's chair and tossed a tightly folded paper on the table in front of me. When I unfolded it, I saw a cartoon drawing of a humanized rat torn from *Time* magazine. Written under the cartoon in the girl's distinctive handwriting was "Aileen." I stared at the cartoon, unbelieving. I'd sometimes been compared to a cartoon rabbit. I well-remembered that Uncle Pat had called me the ugliest child he ever saw. But a human rat? I could not take it in. Without looking up at the sniggering group, I refolded the paper and slipped it in my pocket. Next morning, Quinton wrote a note apologizing for their behavior, not mentioning the drawing. His kind note did not soothe my heart. And that heart was the problem. I staunchly refused to let it be wounded, but sometimes it remained impervious to my protection.

Nonetheless, when we graduated a few days later, I took with me more bright than dark memories of high school, especially of my teachers. I treasured the essay my English teacher, Sarah Faucett, returned to me with her note, "Have you considered becoming a writer?" That was too far-fetched a dream for even me in those Great Depression days but what a thrill to think of such a possibility. Louise Mustin made history real to me. She told us of her ancestor, US President John Tyler. She had known one of Tyler's daughters, although the woman was quite elderly at the time. When Mrs. Mustin described the poverty and devastation her young grandfather-to-be found on returning home to Alabama after Appomattox, I was there! And with Mrs. Blanton, I sailed to Europe on the *Aquitania*, dancing late every night and eating delicious food at all hours. In my imagination, with her I took a boat trip up the Rhine River, toured a castle, and saw the Passion Play. Her favorite country in Europe, clean, friendly Germany, became mine.

I yearned to live such a life, and I was greedy for a college education where I would learn everything known. Yet I had nightmare fears of the WORLD.

Daddy would not accept that.

Hard-pressed financially though we were, he was determined to see that his daughters acquired a college education. Already he had investigated several government programs for Francys who had graduated from high school in 1936 and Jane in 1937. While waiting for developments, my sisters found part-time work, commuting with Daddy who at that time worked a temporary job with a building contractor in Tuscaloosa. Transportation was essential now because as timekeeper and paymaster he had several building sites to visit daily. But soon after the move to Brookwood, we had been forced to sell our Model T to feed our milk cows. Now Daddy went to Tuscaloosa in search of a vehicle for himself and my sisters. He was gone all day. We were in suspense till almost dark. The Delco batteries were down, and we had no gasoline to power them, so we had no lights. I was hanging up the dishpan behind the stove when we heard "Shave and a Haircut, Six Bits" played on a car horn.

"Daddy! He's coming!" we shouted and ran for the backyard just as he drove a Model A Ford in and parked. He bought it for $125, he told us; the inside lining hung in shreds and one door was stuck shut. No matter to us—we were so thrilled to have a car again that we spent most of the first day of possession sitting in it. Besides that, we gloated over the wonderful things he brought us: cakes, crackers, pork and beans, salmon, puffed rice, bran, and more. He even went by the drugstore and got Francys's Kodak pictures she had made of her graduation.

Having the car enabled us to attend the farmers' annual picnic in Tuscaloosa. People gathered in the late-summer shade of the huge pine trees at Verner Elementary School on Tenth Street. Two rows of long tables had a wide space between them where eight big black wash pots of Brunswick stew, one for each section of tables, were fired up. I wrote in my diary: "The chef was a big man with a large bay window stomach emphasized by the white apron he wore. Two men built the fires, kept them burning and stirred the Brunswick stew while the cooks mixed up another pot full. Whew, and was some of it hot! It had corn, butter beans, beef, chicken, tomatoes, okra, squirrel." Delicious! After the ten barrels of lemonade had been consumed—I didn't get a taste of it, but I heard many say how delicious it was—and the political speeches had been made out of the backs of trucks, the farmwomen unpacked their baskets. A very old man gave thanks then the eating began . . . and such eating! I'd never seen so much food as was spread on those two long tables, so appetizing and beautiful, and such a variety—thick, golden pineapple on top of a long brown cake, a big bowl of potato salad with grated egg yolk on top, piles of corn on the cob dripping butter, the brownest, meatiest, tenderest fried chicken to go with Mama's biscuits, fine-textured yellow cake with white icing and hickory nuts sprinkled on top, custards dotted with swirls of

A twice-a-day chore: Aileen's sister Mary Alice carries drinking water from the spring to the house. Aileen's little brother, William (called Buddy), is on the porch at left. (The University of Alabama Libraries Special Collections)

whipped cream, lemon pie with lightly browned meringue, coconut cakes, peach pickles, devil's food cakes, doughnuts in muscadine jelly, coconut pie, apple pie with cinnamon, tea cakes, and tomato sandwiches on homemade bread. Everything you could think of was there and I didn't go over half the tables. Quite a few people who weren't farmers came; I could tell by how they dressed and how they talked and by their loaded plates. I heard one of them say, "Oh, I do want a piece of that delicious sweet bread," so I took a piece too to find out what sweet bread was like, but it was ordinary corn bread.

The farmers' picnic was a grand finale to my unemployed days. My turn to go to work had come but I stubbornly dragged my feet. Knowing how poor we were strengthened my position. Even if I could find a job, it would pay a dollar or less a day. What I did at home was worth more than that. If I had a job, who would cut wood for the kitchen stove? Who would feed the calves? Doctor them when they were hurt or sick? Clean the stalls and spread the manure on the garden? Watch over the chickens, feed and water them, and bring in those valuable eggs? Take the cow down to the corner of the field to graze and keep her out of the corn? Go into the woods twice a day with Mary Alice to bring drinking water from the spring?

No matter—Daddy kept alert for every opportunity.

"There's a chance you all can get on with the National Youth Administration," he explained. "President Roosevelt has fixed it so young people can work while they go to school. I'll have to find out more about that."

By this time Jane's temporary job clerking at McLellan's Five and Ten Cent Store had become full-time. She was well satisfied and decided to stay with it. That was all right with Daddy, but as soon as he could, he took Francys and me to the NYA office to see Mrs. Gardner who was in charge. Her first question disposed of me.

"How old are you?"

"Seventeen," I said, already seeing myself on a college campus, I didn't care which one, studying in the library with a stack of books.

"Oh, you're too young," she said and turned to Francys.

While she and Francys talked, I sat in an outer room, stewing and berating myself for not lying. It would have been so easy to say "Eighteen," though eighteen was yet a year away for me. Later when I was still grumbling about my stupidity, Daddy told me that Mrs. Gardner had records showing the ages of all our family members.

"Besides," Daddy said, "you don't want to ever lie."

I knew within my greedy soul that I wanted that college education so much that I would have lied.

NYA accepted Francys. Plans were made for her to attend the State Teachers' College in Livingston. We knew she would make a good teacher and we were all glad. Mama got out her store of remnants and began sewing for a school wardrobe.

But Daddy wasn't through with me. "You can go to the employment office. There's a chance they'll have something."

After he had taken so much trouble with me, I felt guilty and finally went to the employment office by myself. I made no progress but went home satisfied that I had tried. However, as soon as Daddy had a chance, he took me back there and got me an interview with a Mr. Roth. After some questions, he handed me a card and instructed me to go see the manager at Kress Five and Ten Cent Store, one of the largest of the four dime stores in Tuscaloosa.

The Kress building on Greensboro Avenue not only looked old with its high dark ceilings and dim lights; it smelled old. A self-assured clerk pointed out the manager, Mr. Skelton, and I approached him, trembling. I don't know what I said or how I answered his questions, but he continued working with something on the counter and hardly looked at me, which made the interview a bit easier. Afterwards, I went to the nearby McLester Hotel and sat in the lobby to collect myself until the family came to pick me up.

Almost a month passed with no word from Kress. The threat to my secure world faded in the joy of caring for three new baby calves we adopted from the dairy in Tuscaloosa, two girls (one dollar each) and one boy (free). I was teaching them how to drink milk from a bucket and how to stop bawling for their mothers.

I was unprepared when Daddy drove in from work one late afternoon and Francys and Jane spilled out of the car shouting.

"Aileen, you're to go to work at Kress!"

"Tomorrow! Eight o'clock!"

Everybody rejoiced for me but I almost fainted. Tomorrow! No time to hide, no time to get sick. I could hardly eat a bite at supper. The family went to bed but I stayed up late, trying to forget what faced me tomorrow by twisting the radio dial.

Just as I had decided to switch off the power and go to bed (I was sure I wouldn't sleep a wink), a voice spoke out of the radio, a man's voice, so pleasant I stopped to listen. He was reading a poem:

Sleep sweet within this quiet room
Oh, thou, whoe'er thou art.
And let no mournful yesterday
Disturb thy peaceful heart.
Nor let tomorrow mar thy rest
With dreams of coming ill.
Thy Maker is thy changeless friend,
His love surrounds thee still.

The voice seemed to be in the same room with me and went straight to my troubled heart. Instantly, my whole being was at peace. I snapped off the radio and crept to bed where I slept the rest of the night.

42

The next day, Daddy saw to it that I got to work on time. I was directed upstairs to the office where several other new clerks and Miss Hamner, one of the floorwalkers, were gathered.

"Miss O'Quinn is in charge of the office," Miss Hamner began. "You'll check your purse in with her while you're at work. Do not take any money with you on the Floor. You will always wear dresses and stockings; be sure your seams are straight and that you have no runs."

She showed us the lounge, a large room furnished with two chairs, a stool, a table, and a cot, all looking dingy and hard used.

"Here's where you can eat your lunch and rest while you wait for the bell to go to work."

We followed her downstairs to the Floor where we had lessons in using the cash register and how to treat customers.

"And when you sell an item, right away you refill its space from the understock. Never let a space stay empty."

Another strict rule: "You may not call each other by first names. Always use 'Miss.'" And so I became for the first time "Miss Kilgore."

The one exception to the first-name rule was our Black porter, Harry Postell, whom we addressed as "Harry."

Miss Hamner gave us a warning: "Be on the watch for pilferers, shoplifters. They are clever and cost Kress money. Don't you try to handle any problem. Notify a floorwalker right away if you suspect somebody."

We were then assigned to a counter. I thought I had no preference: hosiery, dry goods, toilet goods, candy, stationery, notions, toys, crockery, jewelry—it didn't matter. But I was assigned to hardware, of all things. In dismay I surveyed tools, tools, tools, and paint, dishpans, slop jars, and grotesque things that had no name and no purpose as far as I was concerned. I did not realize that I was in for an education more useful than anything I'd had in school.

The head hardware clerk came over to meet me. I was astonished to see her—Frances Goins! Back in eighth grade at Brookwood School, we had been good friends. After she was transferred to a different school, I hadn't seen her again. But I hadn't forgotten her kindness or her dimpled smile, both of which she still possessed. If I needed any proof that my Maker was my changeless friend, I had it! She was one

Employees at the Tuscaloosa Kress Dime Store in 1941: (back row, left to right) *Mr. O'Brian, Miss Powell, Miss Burns, Miss Pridmore, Mr. May, Miss Falls, Miss Goins, Mr. Thomas, Harry Postell;* (middle row, left to right) *Miss Ashley, Miss Ewing, Miss O'Quinn, Mr. Skelton, Miss Hamner, Miss Woodward, Miss McDaniel, not remembered;* (front row, left to right) *not remembered, Aileen Kilgore, Miss Hogue, Miss Armand, not remembered, not remembered, Miss Hall, not remembered.*

of the reasons I could write in my diary a few days later: "I did not hate the work at Kress after all. I enjoyed it immensely with the exception of the sore and aching legs and the blistered feet. And when we get home at night I'm just too tired to move. I worked Saturday, Monday, Tuesday and Wednesday and now go back on Saturday again."

I was learning about wrenches (monkey, open end, crescent, and pipe), how to test batteries, the different grades of sandpaper and how each was used, and what was required to paint a dresser. Wrapping the items was a rassle for me, especially slop jars and dishpans. Slop jars, that bedside convenience most country people needed, I learned to call combinettes. We had two kinds, a gray enamel one with no lid for fifty cents and a cream-colored one with a lid for sixty cents. When a customer asked me for a blond slop jar, I could hardly keep from giggling.

I was relieved at how patient customers were with an ignoramus like me, but perhaps it helped that I was eager to learn. Also, most people shared their mishaps and trials in their hardware projects and I had a sympathetic ear.

Making change was not as hard as I expected. In those first days, only one person lost her temper with me, but she explained that my slowness was going to cause her to be late for work. I knew how important a job was and didn't feel hurt.

Not long after I started working at Kress, I was introduced to another aspect of the city—the courthouse. Daddy was called to jury duty. Ordinarily, he was free to take Jane and me home as soon as our stores closed, but one night the jury, in seclusion, couldn't agree. Did a man steal a truckload of poplar logs or not? I sat on that hard courtroom chair waiting, so tired and hungry that I could hardly hold up my head.

I wasn't alone. The man on trial, his wife and children, and several friends sat together; a juryman's son and I sat apart but didn't speak to each other. A few lawyers and court officials, and later the judge, were the only ones moving around.

At 9:30 P.M., I was startled awake by a pounding from inside the jury room. The bailiff sprang up and went to unlock the door. The jury filed out and announced their decision: the man on trial, after hours of deliberation and delay, was found guilty. He was fined one dollar and set free. His family gathered round him rejoicing. I followed Daddy to where he had parked the car and we headed home for a too-short night.

When the business rush of school opening in September was past, I worked only on Saturdays. After the store closed, I would pick up my pay envelope—a dollar bill and twenty-eight cents in change—at the office when I got my purse. By the middle of October, I was still learning—now I knew a coping saw from a hacksaw and how each was used. I'd learned where we kept sparkplugs and that we didn't sell spirit levels. When we clerks waited in the lounge for the bell to return to work, we talked a little but mostly we were glad for the chance to rest and be quiet.

I spent some of my pay to go to the doctor for a hurting that had developed in my side and to the dentist to get my teeth taken care of. The doctor diagnosed neuritis and prescribed a red liquid for me to take (doctor visit, $2.00, medicine, $1.00). The dentist filled three teeth ($3.00); it was a grueling experience because I didn't take Novocain. At previous dental visits, the ripping sound as the needle—dulled by many uses—tore into my gum and the pain of the tearing flesh and bone was more unbearable than the pain of drilling.

As soon as I could, I wanted to get a permanent in my long straight "dishwater blonde" hair. I didn't know anything about beauty shops, but as I walked along the street one morning, I saw a hole-in-the-wall place. Inside sat a young woman, idle, surrounded by the paraphernalia of permanents: bottles, papers, curlers, stands with many wires attached that I knew would electrically bake a curl in my hair.

I went in.

Yes, she could give me a permanent.

When?

Right now.

Fine.

How much?

Two dollars.

In my purse I had two dollar bills, nearly the sum of two long days' work. No matter—I wanted to look better. I sat down in one of her chairs and entrusted myself to her at 8:15 A.M. and did not escape her clutches till 12:30 P.M.

She nearly killed me.

The haircutting was all right. So was the wrapping of each strand in papers and curlers. Even attaching each curler to one of those electric wires was not bad. It was after she had baked me that the pain began—she couldn't comb my curls because my hair was nothing but a tangle. She tore out by the roots almost as much hair as she had cut in the beginning.

I tried to be polite and not cry but tears rolled down my hot cheeks, and I could not stifle the exclamations of pain. Finally, she went to the phone and called someone for advice. I realized that I was her first victim. She put me through all the remedies the advice giver had said—washing my hair in vinegar was the one that finally helped. After desperate work on her part and suffering on mine, I sat in front of a mirror looking at myself while she bragged how pretty my hair was. I didn't have much left.

I paid the two dollars and crept out, wanting to hide my head in a sack. I confided to my diary: "I bought an awful lot of misery with that hard earned two dollars."

Daddy helped me forget my hair disaster when he said, "Want to go with me to Lustig's? That's the only place I can buy a Mobile paper to see where Brother Joe's ship is."

Often I had studied the windows of Lustig's Book and Gift Shop and longed to go inside. I didn't have the courage. I wouldn't know how to act in such a lovely, rich place. But the black-haired woman who greeted Daddy and me smiled a welcome and said, "You're out of luck. A riverboat from Mobile docked here today and the crew came in and bought every copy we had of the Mobile paper."

As far as I was concerned we were *in* luck. Here I was inside surrounded by beautiful books that I could hold and page through: *Old Ships, With Lawrence in Arabia, Forty Famous Ships*, Halliburton's *Flying Carpet*, and more and more. Little bronze fish bookends, star candle holders, silver trays, graceful teapots, lovely compacts, big paintings, handsome writing paper, and softly lit lamps. I inhaled the expensive fragrance of the shop while I read the fine print on boxes of chocolates with names I'd never heard of. My mouth actually watered in an ecstatic dream until Daddy reminded me that we needed to get on the road home.

As our Model A Ford whined along through shabby Peterson and bedraggled Howton, I resolved to pinch my pay even harder and go back to Lustig's. I was giddy with power, the power of having money to spend, money that could get me inside a place like Lustig's. When he could squeeze out a dime, once in a while Daddy bought a magazine, *The Shadow*, for the two of us. The stories were about a mysterious crime fighter with a chilling laugh whose refrain was "The Shadow knows." Now, after this peek into Lustig's, *The Shadow* was a fast-fading memory.

A call from the Frisco Railroad came for Daddy to go to Amory,

Mississippi. He had to borrow five of my last ten dollars to take care of his room and board while he was away. He wrote us that he found a boardinghouse where he paid $1.40 a day for three meals and a bed. He hoped the stint in Amory would be short and that he'd be back in time to take Francys for opening day of school at the State Teachers' College in Livingston.

When Daddy came home he worked over the car: "Bushing up the front end and putting brakes all around," he said. He was confident it would get to Livingston and back. I made up my mind that if the car had room for me I'd go too and see that college. Francys's friend, Nolen, was working hard hauling coal day and night for Joe Avery's mine in Howton, but he took time to come by the house to tell her goodbye, covered with coal dust though he was. He looked exhausted. All through the night before she left, he blared his coal truck horn every time he passed our house. That probably helped him stay awake but it surely disturbed our sleep.

The next day, I squeezed myself into the back seat among suitcases and boxes and gazed out the window in wonder to see countryside new to me—large houses far across level pastures, strange cattle with humps on their backs and low-hanging dewlaps, many horses and mules. The school campus was beautiful, but it was the smell of the classrooms—books and chalk, and learning—that set me on fire. I made sure to get inside the library and look at all those books. Many of them seemed to deal with Southern history and Southern folklore. My hands itched to get hold of them all. Nowhere was my greedy nature more evident than when I was among books. I felt awed as I stood there looking and thinking of Miss Julia Tutwiler in our history book who did so much for our state. She founded this school that my sister was enrolling in to become a teacher. She helped our poor people (that included most of us) and those in prison. I was thrilled to be there and so glad for Francys.

We helped this first sister leaving the nest to unpack her belongings and left her talking with her roommate who seemed to be another nice country girl. We were well satisfied with Francys's situation, and I was already plotting a visit to her. The letters that she wrote in the following days made me even more eager to see her college again. She wrote often telling about the winter clothes (including a pair of shoes) the NYA issued them, and the plentiful, good food in the school dining hall. In our letters to her, we always included a small treat—a stick of gum, a dime, or a letter from Buddy. Mama urged her to be sure and go to church.

Daddy was away again when a check for $55 for past railroad work came in the mail. Most of it had to go for bills we owed: grocery bills ($10), house payment ($16), insurance ($10), etc. Nonetheless, we begged Mama to take us to town. Aunt Mittie was visiting us, but she was too busy filling us in on what Pickensvillians had said about us after our last visit there to have a say-so: all of our cousins, aunts, and uncles agreed that Jane was beautiful, Mary Alice was on the way to being even more beautiful, and Buddy (or Hop Toad as Aunt Mittie liked to call William) was a perfect boy, and Cousin Charlie thought Francys was beautiful. Nobody seemed to notice who was left out as, to our delight, Mama's doubts about taking the car on the road were weakening. Her reasons for staying home were valid: first, she had no license to drive; second, she had done very little driving; and third, the car had regressed into shaking spells. At the most public places, it would begin rattling and shaking so hard I thought my teeth would come loose. And while we waited for the shakes to finish, all we could do was look back at the people who passed and stared.

In spite of all this, Mama gave in finally, and Mary Alice, Buddy, Aunt Mittie, and I settled ourselves in the car, confident Mama would get us there. Down the road a piece, Mama said, "I'd better stop for some gas at Mr. Best's store." At the gas pump, she had to back up and come forward a time or two before parking, but that gave elderly Will Best time to come out to serve us. Ola Best came too and they all were having a good chat, Mama telling them of her uncertainty about driving to town. A man walked up, standing between Mama and the Bests without speaking.

Mr. Best said, "Here's a man wanting to go to town. If you're scairt why don't you let him drive you?"

Mama looked the man up and down. "Who is he?"

Mr. Best said, "Mr. Hogg's son-in-law."

We rearranged our seating, Buddy on the edge of the back seat so he could see, me scrunched between Aunt Mittie and Mary Alice, Mama on the front seat to oversee Mr. Hogg's son-in-law who situated himself under the steering wheel, and we were off with a jerk. He still hadn't said a word. I wondered if he could talk.

The car behaved very well, no shaking, no rattling, but on this day it chose to stop dead on the long, uninhabited stretch of road just before Peterson. Mr. Hogg's son-in-law offered no suggestion for solving our problem though he did get out and walk around the car.

What to do? We just sat there until I unlimbered myself and saw in the woods below the road a man bending over a stream. I went down through bramble briars, trying to protect my stockings, and accosted him. It was Skeeter Mathus. We weren't acquainted but we knew who each other was.

He said, "I'm seining minnows for bait to go fishing," indicating a bucket of water and a seine.

I told him our problem and he agreed to look at the engine. He tinkered under the hood a few minutes while we waited anxiously. I couldn't see what he did but he charged Mama fifty cents. We all hopped in while the motor was running and took off. We got to Tuscaloosa where we parked first at Jitney Jungle to buy a few groceries, the most important thing on our list. Mr. Hogg's son-in-law disappeared right away.

When we reassembled ourselves with flour, baking soda, grits, and some meat scraps for soup, the car wouldn't start. A man passing by got it going for a dime. Mama was so angry over the half dollar she'd paid Skeeter that she could hardly stop fussing and give her attention to town.

I had brought along the last five dollars from my money box in case I should find some cheap shoes as it was Dollar Day all over town. I spent every bit: two pairs of shoes at two dollars each—one an aristocratic Sunday pair, thin soled and tan, the other clodhoppers for work—and a birthday gift for Mary Alice who was still in high school. Five dollars gone with the wind. But the thrill of owning two pairs of new shoes, especially those suede aristocrats, was worth much more to me than four dollars.

Before dark, we gathered at the car again and arranged ourselves.

Buddy, worn out with the excitement of town, leaned on Aunt Mittie. The car started fine, but in backing out Mama cut the wheel too quick and our bumper got tangled in the neighboring car's bumper. It took all of us, including the Hop Toad, to lift our auto and get us free. All went well from then on, with Aunt Mittie saying her prayers all the way home, till Mama turned in at our lane. Again she cut the wheel too quick and the car hung up on the culvert. Gunning the motor and backing and twisting the steering wheel couldn't get us loose. Finally we all lifted the car again, and Mama drove on up the lane while the rest of us walked behind in case the car needed a push to get it safely into the backyard.

My solace that night was the Sunday-go-to-meeting shoes I'd bought for two dollars. I could hardly keep my eyes off them as they sat on the floor under my bed, but my poor feet were so sore I doubted I could wear them anywhere. I also needed a new pair of twenty-five-cent stockings. Those I'd been wearing for three weeks steady, washing them out at night, had holes in the feet and were plastered up at the heels with moleskin to protect my blistered feet. But it was a while before any of us nagged Mama to take us to town again.

The last week in October 1938 I worked from Wednesday through Saturday and drew my biggest pay envelope so far—$6.26. But there would be no visit to Lustig's: Buddy, with winter coming on, needed shoes and Mary Alice had no coat; I wanted two false teeth fitted in the vacancy at the front of my mouth that prevented me from smiling ($50), and the doctor said I ought to have my tonsils removed ($35). Even more important, the car, our Essential, had to have a professional overhaul and a new tag, or we couldn't get on the road.

On the night of October 30, 1938, about 7:25, Daddy and I were listening to Charlie McCarthy on the radio. The static was deafening so Daddy was changing stations when I heard an announcer say, "Here's a special bulletin from the press radio bureau." Daddy was turning the dial further but I asked him to turn back as I had heard it was something about war. The announcer was saying, "I take you now to . . . [a burst of static] . . . where the army is defending the land from the invaders." He said something about enemy airplanes bombing cities and killing thousands. He gave bulletins from Langley Field,

Virginia, and described the havoc being wrought by the approaching enemy. It was horribly real and made cold shivers run up my back. When someone entered the studio, the announcer said, "Just a moment, ladies and gentlemen." He talked excitedly aside for a moment then made some momentous announcement. I knew it couldn't be real because all networks would be carrying reports, and they weren't. As the static was bad, Daddy soon turned back to Charlie McCarthy, and I forgot the war program. Later that night I heard Walter Winchell repeat twice on his news segment, "Ladies and gentlemen, there has been no catastrophe in New Jersey." That meant nothing to me until I saw the next day's newspaper headline: "Too Realistic Radio Program Panics Nation." That was what we'd heard—Orson Welles's too realistic Halloween program, "War of the Worlds."

No one at Kress mentioned the program the next day; we were caught up not only in the Halloween rush but in school openings.

One day I was waiting for a customer and her daughter to choose a wastebasket for the daughter's dorm room at the university. I recognized her as Lily Atkinson, one of Daddy's cousins, prominent in Tuscaloosa. I had met her at Great-uncle Charley Kilgore's funeral. Uncle Charley had been one of two Confederate veterans left in Tuscaloosa County in January 1938 when he died. His funeral was at the First Presbyterian Church with a large turnout of relatives I had never seen before and never saw again. I especially remembered Mrs. Atkinson and her kind husband. Now while I listened to the mother and daughter debating the merits of the wastebaskets, I wondered what they'd say if they knew the young woman leaning on the gray combinette was kin.

For that matter, all my customers would probably be astonished at what was in my mind as I waited for them to make a decision. A man debating the merits of Kress's brand of paint against the national brand we carried would never suspect that I was with a camel train in the Arabian desert: "Somewhere upon that trackless wide, it may be we shall meet The Ancient Prophet's caravan, and glimpse his camel fleet."

Early in December, I began working every day for the Christmas rush. During all the busyness, one of my repeat customers invited me to "go to the show" with him. Being asked out to the movies was a situation Miss Hamner hadn't covered, but I wasn't tempted as there just wasn't time in my life to fit in such an occasion. At the time I seldom gave a thought to my appearance beyond my job's requirements. It was the job that took my whole attention and energy. I was learning new things every day, maybe not the adventurous things I yearned for but business things and people things that I needed in my work. One of the most difficult was making out the daily order. I had to estimate the items I'd sell that day and order replacements for the next. Just before closing time each day, my order arrived in a big basket pulled by a stock boy. Then I had the dual task of putting away the order in the proper places under the counter while continuing to wait on customers. As I learned the business side of my work, I also had to understand the items I was selling and convey that understanding to the customer. In other words, learn salesmanship. The conversing part, to relate to strangers, was difficult for me at first. It came to me only gradually as I realized how interesting and different most of the people were and what amazing things they could tell me.

But some of them overdid it. At a display of baskets one day, I got entangled with a fellow who was in love with basket making. He told me every detail of making baskets and pointed out the many faults of those I had to sell. I paid close attention at first, but when he began criticizing my product, I thought I'd never get rid of him.

When Kress put chocolate-covered cherries, one of our family's favorites, on sale for twenty-five cents, I took home a box. After supper that night, we ate them all while we laughed over Brother Wooley's Sunday prayer request: he had meant to ask God to bless the BYPU (Baptist Young People's Union) but said instead, "Bless the WPA." I told Mama and Daddy they should have said a hearty "AMEN."

Well, we paid more than a quarter for those cheap chocolates; they gave us nightmares. Mama dreamed that Buddy fell in the well, I dreamed I broke my glasses, and Mary Alice dreamed she shot a Japanese soldier out of the rose trellis. Her dream puzzled us. At that time we had no idea of Japanese soldiers or war; where her prophetic dream came from we couldn't figure out.

In mid-1938, I had the wondrous thrill of Howard Hughes's

round-the-world flight. Hughes was a Texan, heir to an oil fortune, and passionate about flying. Never before in my wanderlust dreams had I considered anything except camels and sailing ships. Now I took to the air with Hughes and his crew when they left Burbank, California, on the way to New York to begin the flight, and I hardly left the radio until they returned. I jotted notes as I listened to updates so I could relive the trip later.

The mechanics in New York had a great deal of trouble with the motors, especially the right one, before "lanky, taciturn" thirty-two-year-old Hughes and his crew walked out of the hangars just a few minutes before the takeoff on July 10. Mrs. Thurlow, wife of the navigator, Thomas Thurlow, called to her husband, "God speed you, sweetheart, and happy landings." The takeoff lasted forty-five seconds. Three hours later I heard Richard Stoddart, the radio operator, broadcast an update. He said the trip was uneventful but they were using more fuel than they had expected. The plane was 470 miles out and they were traveling at 155 miles per hour. Hughes also talked. His voice was flat and rather nasal and he did not speak as well as Stoddart.

A news flash told me that the ocean liner *Île de France* reported that the plane was nearing the French coast. Arriving in Paris after sixteen and a half hours in the air, Hughes was the first to alight, pausing to put on a necktie and his battered brown hat. One reporter described him as "tousled haired and fatigued." The US ambassador to France, Mr. Bullit, greeted him with a hug, as did an air ace who had met Charles Lindbergh in 1927.

After a sip of champagne and three bites of steak, Hughes had trouble at takeoff before becoming airborne for Moscow. One observer, after witnessing the perilous efforts to get aloft, said, "That guy must have a horseshoe in his pocket."

After Moscow, Hughes continued to Siberia, then Fairbanks, Alaska, where they were met by Mrs. Wiley Post—I well remembered how we'd grieved when Daddy came home from the store one day in 1935 and said that Wiley and Will Rogers had crashed and died at Point Barrow, Alaska.

Hughes's plane left Fairbanks almost immediately for Minneapolis and then New York. Howard was still wearing his battered brown hat on arrival and was greeted by a huge crowd including Jacqueline Cochrane, champion woman aviator, and Dick Merrill. Before Hughes even made an appearance the crowd was screaming, "Howard! Howard!" There was so much shouting, so much band playing, so much racket and clamor coming through the radio that I could barely hear the police shouting, "Put down that camera! Put down that camera!" Mrs. Thurlow, encircled by policemen, was pushing through the crowd trying to reach her husband. She gasped to the announcer, "This crowd is mashing my tongue out."

The reception for the flyers, held on July 15, was a humdinger. The newscaster said Hughes was very nervous, biting his lip and looking paler than usual. He got up in a funk, the announcer said, because he knew what was in front of him. He wore a blue suit and clutched his brown hat in one hand. Occasionally he waved to the crowd with the other hand. He muttered under his breath to Mr. Whalen, New York's mayor, who tried to soothe him. The announcer hopped on the running board and asked Hughes to say a word. Hughes said "Hello" in that flat Texas drawl, and that was all. The announcer added that he had never seen anything to equal that motorcade and the millions milling about. "It looks like a snowstorm," he said, "what with all the confetti, ticker tape, torn-up telephone books, and so forth." Someone on Wall Street threw a roll of ticker tape down and failed to remove it from the metal roller. It hit a motorcycle cop, knocking him off his motorcycle. He narrowly escaped serious injury.

When the time came for Hughes to speak, he was so terribly nervous I sympathized with him. He said, "I'm very nervous as you've probably noticed and I'm not expressing very well what I want to say but I hope you understand." He also said that reporters had taken his speech away from him. He had a paper to go by during the first part but he had to improvise the last part. I thought he did well considering all the hubbub and chaos going on around him.

Hughes had flown around the world in ninety-one hours, breaking Wiley Post's time and setting a new record.

From all that excitement, I came down to earth pretty quick getting back to work. The first Saturday, as I returned from supper hour, a special gift for me materialized out of the gray winter shadows. Tottering toward me near the Kress door was a cat, very thin and very old. I greeted him and he answered. I recognized he was homeless and in need, and he was my favorite color for cats, gray with black stripes. How could I leave him on that cold dark street? I patted him, signifying that he should wait, I'd be back. At Miss Thompson's counter I asked her for a large yarn box with a lid and some of her old yarn scraps for a soft bed. In the sides and top of the box I poked breathing holes with the scissors I kept in my purse. Then gently I laid the willing cat inside. His frame was so large that he covered the bottom of the box. "What a giant you must have been in your heyday," I said softly. Now for Harry, our porter, the solver of any problem. I asked him to keep my cat in the basement till the store closed. Then, after Miss O'Quinn checked the contents of the box, I loaded my cat into our Model A. I held the box in my lap to comfort him during his first automobile ride but he never made a sound. During the fifty minutes it took for us to reach home, he and I silently agreed on his name— Samuel Kress. Our resident cats made no objection to him joining them, probably because they realized he wasn't able to offer them any competition.

Later in 1938, with Christmas coming near, the railroad called Daddy to work at Adamsville, Alabama. On payday morning, he had no money to buy breakfast but he told the café man he was the Frisco telegrapher and would be paid later that day. He asked for credit but the man refused. How devastated I felt knowing my father went hungry on Christmas Eve. As soon as he got his paycheck, he mailed it to us and the railroad sent him to Tupelo, Mississippi.

At the store, we were busy every minute. With all the crowds and the noise it was hard to keep good sense. But in another way it was exhilarating to be so busy. Christmas Eve was the busiest day, and after the store closed, we weary workers toted everything on the Floor upstairs and everything upstairs down to the Floor, or so it seemed to me. Every Christmas item—cards, toys, and all—had to be carefully packed away for next year. As each clerk left for the night, the manager gave her a bag of fruit. Miss Thompson, whom I especially admired for her know-how and her knowledge of our merchandise, surprised me with the beautifully wrapped gift of a silk scarf.

January 1939 Daddy was still in Tupelo. He wrote us about the trouble he was having with his boarding places: first, he discovered he was living with a thief in the house. He moved, but his new place was infested with green flies and over a saloon that celebrated both day and night. From there, he found a room that seemed to be okay until he discovered he shared it with two big dogs—they slept in his bed while he was at work. Tired of moving, he decided to stay with the dogs for the time being.

My first big lesson of the New Year at work was learning about counter stretchers. Miss Thompson was remaking a counter. She had it all torn up and seemed to be struggling with putting it back together.

"This just won't fit," she said. "Run ask Mr. McKibbon for the counter stretcher."

Eager to help, I found Mr. McKibbon, a floorwalker, changing window decorations. He looked taken aback at my request but said, "Mr. Graves might know. Ask him."

I sped downstairs to the basement to find Mr. Graves, assistant floorwalker. He said, "I haven't used it. Ask Harry."

Harry was on the street washing windows. He stopped and looked at me. "Miss Kilgore, they're fooling you. No such thing as a counter stretcher."

How dumb I felt. I should have suspected they were having fun sending me on a wild goose chase. I trudged back to Miss Thompson who was grinning.

"They don't know where it is," I said. "Somebody must have pilfered it." We laughed and that was the end of it.

In June 1939 time seemed to me to be flying, mostly because I was working steadily. As each regular salesgirl went on vacation (usually for two weeks), the manager asked me to take over her counter. I was glad as it gave me experience on nearly every counter in the store.

Hosiery was the one counter I hated: "Saturday! What an awful day!" I wrote in my diary. "I couldn't endure work next week if I knew I'd be on hosiery facing another day like yesterday. Not one minute's breathing space—the counter completely overturned and in some places completely bare. I didn't even get my daily hosiery order put away. How I got the order made is a mystery to me."

For some time I had been thinking of buying a tube of Max Factor lipstick, one dollar at the drugstore. Kress's brand of lipstick cost ten cents, but I longed for the heavy gold case with the famous makeup man's lipstick inside. I yearned to carry around a little bit of Hollywood magic in my purse. A year ago, I would never have had such a wild thought, but now when I spread my savings out on the bed I counted $43.30! I could faintly remember how thrilling it was when my little money box held eighty-five cents. I thought and thought for several days, struggling with myself, before gritting my teeth, marching into Taylor's Drugstore, and buying the lipstick. When Mama, always practical, saw it, she said, "You paid ninety cents for that brass holder and a dime for the lipstick."

Every day enhanced my education in city life. Friends of Jane's who worked with her showed us a new way to flirt one night when they walked with us past the bakery. We girls stood in front of the expansive glass windows to watch the bakers—twenty-five of them at least in their white outfits—kneading the dough and shaping it into rolls and loaves. They seemed to be absorbed in their work until they noticed us spectators. Then they began pinching off lumps of dough and throwing them with a plop against the glass windows that separated us. Some of the dough clung to the glass but other blobs dropped to the floor. The prettiest got the most blobs. All of us maintained serious expressions as if we were studying the intricacies of bread making but that didn't stop the showers of dough balls. When we moved on I said, "I bet they scrape up that dough and add it back into the loaves and rolls."

The town girls discounted that but even so this curious custom didn't appeal to me. My loves were still books. To my wish list for Lustig's I had added Anne Morrow Lindbergh's *Listen! The Wind* and *The Letters of T. E. Shaw.* I longed to lounge on the veranda of Shepheard's Hotel in Cairo, watching Lawrence of Arabia coming in along with desert sheiks. Of course, I knew Lawrence had died on his motorcycle in 1935, but that was no obstacle to my imagination.

Though my dreams wandered the world, I still appreciated home. On a Sunday in midsummer of 1939, I realized how much I had missed by working so steadily at my job. I saw my first June bug of the year hovering over Mama and Buddy's flower garden while we peeled peaches in the shade of the house. The Elberta peaches were so perfectly ripe that we took the peeling off without a knife, leaving them mealy and golden. We also had two new pigs (a bargain at $1.25 each) that I had not seen before. Looking out the upstairs windows, I saw that the neighbor's plowed fields across the lane were especially beautiful—soft red shading into deep brown, the furrows crawling around the slight rise toward the Smith house. The mellow voices of the Black workers, giving orders to the mules or singing, blended with the sweet high-pitched song of the meadowlarks.

Daddy was in Nettleton, Mississippi, with his part-time railroad work. "A real nice job," he wrote us. "I don't work on Sundays or holidays." He urged Mama and Buddy to come visit him. He'd been gone so long that I knew he was homesick as he was a real homebody. Without giving a reason, Mama refused to go. At last Daddy was able to come home.

As he could type, the WPA now transferred him from the roadwork truck to the WPA project at the University of Alabama. He typed manuscripts seventy-two hours a month at sixty-seven cents an hour, equaling $48.24 per month. How we rejoiced to have the assurance of that certain income. Even more, we were glad for Daddy to have easier working conditions. In addition, each day he picked up several coworkers for thirty cents a ride. One of them, Mrs. Lancaster, gave him stacks of magazines she subscribed to, including *House Beautiful*, *House and Garden*, and *Ladies Home Journal*. I gloated over the beautiful houses and lovely rooms, studying the plans and changing them around as if they were mine. Monogrammed linens, ice blue tablecloths, exquisite glassware, furniture, china, and silverware, like the things I'd seen at Lustig's, stirred my yearnings. Ah me!

Daddy asked his supervisor, Ben, to save his copies of the Birmingham newspapers (the *Birmingham News*, the *Post*, and the *Age-Herald*)

*Aileen's parents,
Annie Gertrude
Cox and William
Oscar Kilgore,
while courting.*

for us too. It didn't matter to me how old the news was when I read it—I was still interested, and the funny papers were never out of date. Odd McIntyre's column always intrigued me and I laughed to read about his transcontinental train trips. All the way from New York to California, as he lay in his berth, he listened to the train wheels clacking: "He shot the dart right through my heart, he shot the dart right through my heart."

With the assurance of a steady income, one of the first things Daddy did was have Mama's engagement diamond reset. Sometime before, as she was sweeping the room, she put the trash, without examining it, directly into the little wood stove called a laundry heater.

The next day, she took up the ashes and dumped them in the old well in the backyard. It was later that she missed her ring. We searched everywhere but couldn't find it. Daddy joined the search, and after examining the house thoroughly, he went out to the well to check for anything there that might possibly be her ring. Sure enough, he found it, the gold all melted but the diamond intact. Now he had it reset as a gift to Mama. Few things thrilled Mama, but her new ring did. She wrote Francys who was still at the State Teachers' College in Livingston: "I can't do much for looking at my ring. I got it Saturday and it's very pretty."

We were well aware of events in Europe as they moved toward what would become World War II. A man in Germany named Adolph Hitler seemed determined to gobble up every country in Europe and clamp down on them with no regard to the rights of the citizens. I remembered that my teacher, Mrs. Blanton, had told our class that when she traveled in Europe years earlier Germany was her favorite country; it was the most beautiful of all and the people were the cleanest and friendliest. What had happened? Daddy supplemented my funds so I could subscribe to *Time* and *Life* magazines. From them I learned that many young people in the small countries under threat from the Nazis were listening to a song called "Gloomy Sunday" and then committing suicide. I wanted to hear that song; I tried and tried to find it on the radio but I never could. We listened to Hitler's speeches on the radio in astonishment. He seemed insane to me, ranting, raving, frothing at the mouth. But then I thought of the many preachers I had suffered through who had acted the same way. What a horror!

Uncle Joe had given us the radio a few years before; we preferred listening to its shortwave bands rather than its regular-band stations because shortwave had no static to drown out punch lines or critical sentences in news broadcasts. And I was fascinated to know that the voices I was hearing came from the far corners of the earth. I had written in my diary in July 1937: "No trace of Amelia Earhart though they have the *Lexington* and *Colorado* looking for her." I also had noted that we heard the broadcast of the flying boat *Caledonia* landing in

Montreal, proving that commercial transatlantic airmail and passenger service were practical.

Even though we lived on an isolated farm, Daddy taught us to be a part of that vast world and to do so we *had* to vote. "Voting gives us power," he said. "And if you don't vote, you have no right to complain against the government." As each of us came of age, he helped us register and paid our poll tax. He remembered those dark years when he could not pay it and he and Mama could not vote. One of the first things he did when he got a job was to pay the current poll tax and all the back years' amounts, as was required. Now on election days he served at the polls, sometimes as an inspector, sometimes as a supervisor.

————

At Kress, we heard more and more about the new store in our future. It was to be on Main Street, spacious and modern. Part of our stock had already been moved and two of our floorwalkers worked over there all the time getting ready for the opening. That left only Miss Hamner and Harry to carry goods for us. Working alone one day, Harry had a narrow escape.

A breathless woman came in the store and said, "Harry's out there unloading freight and that old elevator door fell on him."

"Oh, is he hurt?" I exclaimed.

"Not much," she said, "but I sure thought he was."

None of us could do without Harry.

————

Sometimes Daddy had to take the car in order to reach a railroad job on time. Then Jane and I bought a five-day book of tickets from the Greyhound bus station in Tuscaloosa, five round trips for $2.25. For the Saturday round trip, we had to pay one dollar each, more than half a day's pay. But of all the new adventures, this was the most wonderful. I would talk to people with odd accents traveling far, and they would ask me about my life and Tuscaloosa's history.

As I had never heard myself before, I learned that I talked different. One man said, "You mean you grow rice here?"

```
Tuesday
May 9, 1939

It's already 9 o'clock and I have to roll up my hair yet. Then I'm going
to crawl in the bed and rest my weary legs and feet. These last two
days seemed to crawl by. Only Tuesday and it seems like a year since
Sunday. I've done better then I expected especially on the orders.
They're easy if you can squeeze in time between customers to make one.

Let me tell you about my first bus ride (last night). It was wonderful.
Daisy and Mr. Walker sat across the aisle from Jane and I. Daisy xxx
xix did something with a little knob to make her chair lean back. I
wanted to fix mine that way but I was afraid to tamper with it. It might
dump me out in the aisle or lower me into the lap of the man behind me.
If either should have happened I was too tired to remove myself either
from the floor or the lap.

The bus rode so easy, sitting high on those soft seats, bumps meant
nothing. No rattling like our tin lizzie.

                                           Aileen

                              The Ten-Cent store Girl
```

Diary entry from when Aileen began working at Kress describing her first bus ride.

"Oh, no," I said. "Grass. Grass for cows."

So I learned that I said "grice" instead of "grass."

Coming home after the day's work was especially thrilling. The bus rode so easy: with us sitting high on those soft seats, bumps meant nothing. And no rattling like our Model A. I sat behind the driver because he kept his large window rolled down to let the soft summer air blow in. But one twilight a bat flew past the driver and smacked against my glasses. "There goes two weeks' work," I thought, for I was sure my glasses broke. They hung askew and were a little bent, but to my relief, they were still all in one piece. I plucked the soft bat off them and tossed it out the window where it took wing and wavered off. When I got home, I doctored two bat bites on my temple and they healed quickly.

There was a tiring drawback to bus riding. Because of the increase in Birmingham commuters when the university was in session, we often had to stand the seventeen miles with nothing to hold on to. Instead of running a second bus, the company crowded seventy-five people into a space meant for thirty-five. That was an unhappy circumstance for a country person who had no other way to get to the doctor as well as for a store clerk who had to stand on her feet all day.

When I was home late afternoons, the Hop Toad and I played games. In one game that we named "cannibals," we pretended to eat chickens, calves, whatever came our way. We had spears and Buddy made us chopsticks to eat our victims with. We also rolled discarded tires; mine was named Geeslan Shinho'ster, and Buddy's was named Foghorn, in honor of his cat. We chased each other and raced dangerously close before swerving. No chicken or cat felt safe in the yard when Buddy and I were playing with tires. We also turned ourselves into airplanes, making noises and flying with our left arm turning like a propeller. Best of all we played fairies, Peter Pan and Wendy fairies *zit, zit, zitting* around the outside of the house.

I promised Buddy a book about Peter Pan. When I went to Lustig's to get a fifty-cent copy, they had just received "a beautiful, new edition" for one dollar. I couldn't resist it.

"Would you like it gift wrapped?" the blonde Miss Lustig asked.

I stood silent. Already I'd paid a half dollar more than I had allowed. Could I afford gift wrapping? Finally I stuttered, "How much will that cost?"

She smiled. "It's free."

Free? Oh, my! Yes!

When she finished, it was lovely—white tissue paper with blue and yellow bows and sunflower seals. Coming out of an exclusive shop with a dollar book wrapped as a gift, I knew the meaning of "walking on air."

Buddy was transported by the book; he studied the illustrations and had me read the story to him over and over. When we played pirates now, the one who was Captain Hook used a coat hanger for the arm the crocodile made off with, and Mama gave us an old clock that didn't keep time anymore but still ticktocked loud enough for our crocodile.

We had fun but I worried because Buddy had no playmates his age. For a time a boy named Ward lived nearby. Buddy's report on their conversations concerned us somewhat, both the vocabulary and the pronouncements. "Ward says calling somebody a liar is not bad, no matter what my teacher says," he told us. "And 'shat' is not anything bad to say either." Before we could invite Ward to attend Sunday school with Buddy, his family moved away.

On his own though, Buddy made a friend that tickled all of us. He noticed a big white truck that drove past our house regularly several times a week. When he heard it coming, no matter what he was doing, he ran to the front porch and waved and waved. The driver noticed him and blew his horn in answer. The driver then began tooting his horn as soon as he came in sight of the house. Buddy quickly learned the sound of the truck's motor and could get to the porch before the driver blew his horn. Their friendship delighted us all. And one day, marvel of marvels, the big white truck turned in our lane and came up our long driveway. Both the man and Buddy were so delighted to see each other that they couldn't talk at first, just beam at each other. The man's name was Mr. Hines; he lived in Birmingham and had a regular job of transporting merchandise between Birmingham and Tuscaloosa.

When he noticed our cow, he asked Mama about butter and buttermilk, and he bought some of both, providing Mama with a bit of change for spending. After that, he was a regular customer so Buddy got to see him at least once a week. All of this resulted from one lonely little boy waving to a passing truck.

I was still having new experiences too, but mine didn't always turn out so happily as Buddy's. A stock boy appeared at my counter one day with a vacuum cleaner. "Miss Thompson says your counter needs cleaning," he informed me. I knew about such cleaners. I had seen the other girls using them. But I had never had anything to do with one myself. I located the button to turn it on. The loud roaring frightened me and the air hose strained to jump out of my grip. I restrained it with both hands and tried to do what I had seen others doing when they used the cleaner. All went fairly well until I noticed how the embroidery thread was disappearing in thin air. Before I understood that the cleaner was swallowing it, a good bit of my day's profit was gone.

Personally, one of my ongoing goals was gaining weight. I wanted to be strong for the tonsillectomy I was saving for. "Eat more, drink more milk" became one of my numerous mottos. I tried store-bought pasteurized milk for the first time and decided it must be the dead germs that made it taste so bad. Hard as I tried I was at a standstill; I couldn't get beyond 96 pounds.

At Easter we stayed open till 9:00 P.M. I was surprised that we were busier than at Christmas. Purses, corsages and boutonnieres, ribbons, and Easter baskets sold so fast we couldn't keep the counters filled. It was taken for granted that every clerk who wasn't busy would help out on any counter swamped with customers. I tried to turn my back on the ribbon counter. I detested measuring one-eighth, one-fourth, three-fourths yards of ribbon and figuring the cost; it was brain straining but I struggled through. There was no time to keep the floor behind our counter clear of empty boxes and other castoffs, no time to sweep the floor. It was so littered with trash that we could hardly squeeze past one another to reach the cash register.

After the store closed, all Easter cards had to be counted and saved for next year. Stuffed rabbits had to be packed away, and our daily order stashed in the correct place in the understock below the counter. Mr. Skelton gave a huge chocolate rabbit to Miss Woodward (candy counter). To all the other regular salesgirls, he gave a leftover Easter lily. The extra lily he gave to me.

I still held on to my dream of college, but in April 1939 the National Youth Administration shut down and the Works Progress Administration was in disarray. When the WPA straightened out, Ben, the supervisor, was fired, and Daddy was put in charge of the typing project. Whereas Ben, with no children and a maid, had been paid $100 a month, Daddy, with the same responsibilities as Ben and five children and no maid, was paid the same $56 a month as before.

We valued income from whatever source we could get it honestly. Buffalo Rock Ginger Ale mounted a large sign on our roadside land with Daddy's permission. One night we heard ripping and tearing and realized somebody was trying to carry away our sign. Daddy roared a threat at the culprit and started down the lane. A car came slowly along and picked up an indistinct figure hurrying away from the sign. The next morning Daddy used a hammer to straighten the damage and re-nail the sign to the posts. "It's time Buffalo Rock paid the year's rent," Daddy said. "We can't do without their two dollars."

Even more eerie than the sign stealer was the car that drove up our lane one night after we were all in bed. It parked outside the dining room windows but nobody inside the vehicle made a move. Daddy put on his shoes and went out while I knelt at the dining room windows where I could see the silhouette of a man at the steering wheel.

"Come on out," the man commanded.

Daddy walked in front of the headlights right up to the driver's window. Suddenly the motor roared, the gears churned, and the car went backward down the lane much faster than it had come up.

Daddy stood in the dark looking down the lane then came inside.

"I didn't recognize who it was," he said, "and I don't know that car."

And we never knew. But I was a long time getting to sleep that night because of the fear in my heart for Daddy's safety.

I had turned eighteen on April 10, and Daddy again took up the pursuit of a college education for me through the NYA, which had revived. I followed him deep into the tobacco-drenched bowels of the courthouse through ten or twelve arches until we came to a corner so dark that we could hardly make out the other folks sitting there.

Daddy, on the bench behind me, leaned forward and whispered every time he thought of something I should or shouldn't say. A woman on the bench with me said that an office worker would pass out numbers and call us in that way.

Sure enough, shortly thereafter a woman came out of the office with little pieces of paper. "Who wants one?" she demanded.

The woman by me leaped forward and so did I. The others waiting just stared at the office worker and she didn't explain. She went back into the office and shut the door. We waited. After a while the employee came out again. "Number one," she called.

The woman next to me was ready. She followed the employee into the office. I sat expectant. Soon number one came out and left without looking at me. I prepared to leap. But the door stayed shut.

Finally I noticed it inching open and a voice said, "Number two. Number two."

I managed my weak knees somehow and got inside. The woman at the desk was all business. She asked lots of questions and then gave me a blank form that a notary public had to sign to prove I was an

American citizen. Since we didn't have fifty cents for a notary public, Daddy went to a woman he knew in the county agent's office and she obliged us.

Back at work, Mr. Skelton asked me if I'd take the dry goods counter for a couple of weeks. I hesitated, thinking of all the fractional measuring and figuring involved. But I loved getting that fat pay envelope every Saturday night.

He said, "It's for you to decide. I have two or three other girls I can ask but I think you can do it better."

"I'll do it," I said. As it turned out, I handled dry goods just fine. I was amused at one customer who asked for a size 54 pattern for her neighbor. She said, "That woman is as big as a bale of cotton."

During that time, I had my first experience eating at a restaurant, Pickle's Place. My desires went beyond the fifteen-cent hamburger I ordered. I coveted one of those packets of cookies with the motto "Nibble a Nab for a Nickel"—but remembering my tonsil fund, I squeezed my nickel tight.

While we ate, we were entertained by the cook in the kitchen complaining about all the worms in the turnip greens she was washing. "Law me! I'm bathing worms instead of washing greens." I was glad we didn't plan to eat supper there.

Work on our farm continued without me. Mama hired Sid, our occasional helper, to dig postholes for a cow pasture. While he was in the kitchen eating dinner, Sid said his brother got drunk and had a fight with an old man over in Lawrence's Bottom, knocking out the old man's false teeth. Later the old man had sent word for Sid's brother to come help him hunt for his teeth. He was too afraid of snakes to search by himself.

Nothing came for me from the NYA visit and the program ended in June. Then woe, woe, Daddy's WPA typing project at the University of Alabama was discontinued. I was sort of prepared for the news from the NYA, but I couldn't bear to think of the coming months without Daddy's paycheck.

Jane continued to be satisfied at McLellan's with no wish for college. She'd been given a raise and even helped out in the office sometimes. She paid Mary Alice and me five dollars to trade rooms with her; we moved upstairs and she took over the back bedroom. She hired John Smith to paint the ceiling white and the walls a robin egg blue; she hung white net curtains over the double windows and spread a white coverlet over her bed. She bought a linoleum rug with rose-colored flowers to match the walls. For the future, she planned to buy pictures to hang on the walls and pretty chairs to set by the windows that overlooked the chinaberry trees. I was thrilled to watch as Jane turned that room into a picture-pretty place like in my magazines.

Then, on a sudden, the Tuscaloosa union called a strike at her store. One night, when we went for Jane, we were shocked to find a crowd, interspersed with policemen, gathered around McLellan's front doors. Several attractive girls, none of them McLellan's employees, had been recruited from somewhere to wear "ON STRIKE" signs. They frolicked up and down the street corner at Broad and Greensboro as if they were in a show.

I was mad, mad, mad. "This puts a sprag in Jane's wheel," I later wrote in my diary. "All her plans for her beautiful room, up the chimney like smoke." Besides that, for the union to strike this store was cowardly; McLellan's was the smallest and weakest of the four dime stores. The union would not have dared to tackle Kress or Woolworth, the giants. I was stewing over all this as we tried to get to the store entrance.

Various voices shouted at us, "Don't go in there—they're on strike."

"Don't be a scab!"

"Support justice, don't buy here!"

A man blocked the door.

"Excuse me, please," I said coldly as we pushed past him to find Jane. She was in the back sorting through dress patterns. No customers were in sight.

"What's going on?" Mama asked.

"Well, you know the management has been complaining about the notions girl," Jane said. "She doesn't keep up her counter and is slow to wait on customers. So this morning the manager fired her. The union was on us like a duck on a June bug. They've been here all day trying to make the store rehire her."

"I don't see how they can do that. It's not the union's store," Francys said.

"They can ruin business as you see," Jane said. "They keep after me to quit but I plan to stay."

Just then a man in baggy trousers sauntered past us and said out of the corner of his mouth, "We'd do the same thing for you girls if you needed protectin'."

"He thinks we're buying something," Mama said.

"I would if I had some money," I said.

"All but four of the girls have quit," Jane said.

I was quick to say, "I hope you don't. I hope you stay with the store."

"It isn't easy. They say such hateful things and they insult the few customers we have."

"How I wish I was rich!" I said. "I'd buy every stocking you've got."

Francys was searching her pockets. "Here's a nickel. Let's buy Buddy some candy."

At the candy counter as we were choosing our five cents' worth, a man needing a little shave, a little bath, a little haircut accosted us.

"The people here are on strike," he said. "I wouldn't buy anything. I wouldn't be a scab."

Jane walked up then and I said to her brightly, "He says he's a scab."

He hunched his shoulders, squared his elbows, and tightened his fists as he came toward me. "I didn't no such!"

"You didn't?" I said and leaned sideways to shake my ear. "I'm a little bit deaf. I surely thought you said you're a scab but I know that's something that covers an old sore."

He snorted and stomped away.

Just outside the store as we got in our car, the pretty girls hollered, "Pardon me, puulleeze," and looked at each other laughing.

I turned to face them. "I'm so glad I taught you all some manners," I said.

One of them shouted, "If I were you I'd go to the barber shop."

The following Sunday afternoon three men appeared at our house, a Mr. Haley, a Mr. Koster, and a Mr. Adair. They asked to talk to Daddy and Jane on the porch but I listened from the living room window. The men harangued the two of them for about two hours trying to make Jane quit, or failing that, to persuade Daddy to make her quit. They claimed among other things that every salesgirl except Jane had quit.

"None of this is propaganda," one of them said. "Every word is the gospel truth."

I could tell that Jane was wavering. After they left she told Daddy, "Maybe I should quit. Would that be best?"

"Let's talk to your manager in the morning and see," Daddy suggested.

The next day, we were too early for any pickets to be about. Mr. Knight, the manager, came out to the car. He was willing to abide by whatever Jane decided but he said, "Weaver is still with us. She's in the store now." That decided Jane as she was long-time friends with Weaver. She went in to work.

But Jane and Weaver finally quit because we were afraid that the union might hinder them finding work elsewhere. The store was doomed, and eventually it gave in to the union's demands. Among the terms of settlement, McLellan's had to rehire the notions clerk; all the clerks who were rehired, Jane among them, had to pay union dues and attend the monthly meetings.

Jane found those meetings disagreeable. "After the dull business is taken care of they turn on the phonograph and want to dance," she said. "Ugh," said Weaver one night while riding home with us. "It's awful dancing with those pussle-gutted old men. And I'm just too tired after working all day. I want to go home." And, of course, Jane didn't know how to dance because we were true-blue Baptists. Later she was chosen as one of the union beauties for their Labor Day parade float. Eventually, the notions salesgirl who had caused the strike was fired anyway with the blessings of the union. She didn't pay her union dues and refused to attend union meetings.

Even so, business for McLellan's never recovered to what it had been before the strike though the store managed to stay open. And Jane seemed to lose heart over her room decoration plans. I regretted that because I still had in my memory the pictures I had studied in the magazines given to us—I'd cut out and kept my favorites. I was sure her room would be just as beautiful.

CHAPTER THREE

IN MIDSUMMER OF 1939 VACATIONS at Kress were almost over and it seemed to be a good time for me to have my tonsils out. I had saved enough money, and Dr. Dawson Shamblin told me that the frequent colds and sore throats I had would lessen with the tonsils removed. On the Big Day, Mama drove me to Druid City Hospital, which at that time was at the edge of the University of Alabama campus. As I lay in bed resting and waiting for the doctor to come, I kept thinking what a lovely day it was and how good I felt. How could I deliberately make myself sick? I wanted to jump out of bed, throw my clothes on, and light out for the country. Gritting my few teeth, I restrained myself, and at ten o'clock two student nurses lifted me onto a little bed with wheels and rolled me to the elevator. The elevator wouldn't work so they rolled me outside and across the hospital driveway to another elevator.

Then we went down a long, wide hallway. I raised up and peered around trying to see all I could before the doctor started cutting on me.

It would have been better if I hadn't looked.

Somebody lay stretched out on a table with a hole in his stomach; it appeared to me that the folks standing around him were poking around in his insides.

The student nurses put me next door to that room, strapped my legs down, tied up my head, and covered my eyes. One nurse held my wrists while the other one put something over my nose. Did it stink! Before long, my legs felt like they were floating around and I seemed to sink down into something soft and black. Then I was a goner.

Mama told us she never saw a doctor so wrung out as Dr. Shamblin when he came in the waiting room later to report to her. "He was red-faced and so soaking wet with perspiration he was dripping."

"The operation went well but Aileen took the ether badly," he told her. "She swallowed her tongue several times. That complicated things." He said I really was a Mama's girl—I called her all the time I was in the operating room.

I wasn't the only one hollering for mama. A small boy in the nearby ward called "Mama!" with every breath. And next door to my room a sixteen-year-old boy delirious with typhoid fever would suddenly bellow in the quiet: "Ma! Oh, Ma!"

Later when Mama saw Dr. Shamblin's older brother, also a doctor, she told him about my experience. "Oh," he said, "I didn't know Dawson did tonsillectomies." So there I was—as with my permanent, another practice subject for someone.

For a while I was feeble but eager to go back to work. As soon as I pushed open the swinging glass doors that Harry polished every day, smelled the buttered popcorn, and heard the bleating of the phonograph, the clash of voices, and above all the sound of cash registers ringing up sales, I felt welcomed. And I fitted in as if I'd never been away.

I was delighted when Miss Armand (toilet goods) invited me to go with her to confession one Saturday supper hour. I knew that she was from Louisiana and attended St. John's Roman Catholic Church. Being an unornamental Southern Baptist, I had heard some scary stories about the Roman Catholic Church. Here was a chance to see for myself. She covered my head with her handkerchief before we entered the dimly lit church. I seated myself while she went through a dark door to the priest. I studied the assortment of people who waited their turn to confess. All of them appeared serious, absorbed in their thoughts. They were much more respectful of their place of worship than we Baptists were, I thought.

I liked Miss Armand but I avoided working on her counter. Pieced-together, one-legged men on crutches regularly came to buy her hair tonics to drink for the alcohol content, since Tuscaloosa was "dry" and liquor couldn't be sold legally. Bay rum was their favorite. The sales-girl was supposed to discourage them from such buying because the kind of alcohol used in those tonics was destroying them. Without exception the men were ingratiating in a desperate way, and oh, so pitiful that I never learned how to bring up the subject of their addiction. Besides, I told myself, they know better than anybody what it's doing to them. They won't listen to me.

By August 20, 1939, we had had the grand opening of the new store. What a great day! I worked on one of the two notions counters and was afterwards given the gorgeous bouquet that adorned it.

"It's your counter," Miss Thompson assured me. That's all the word I got and I could hardly believe it. A regular girl! I'd be paid on Tuesday nights instead of Saturdays. I'd be fixed in one place, not swapping around and adjusting to all the other counters.

Actually, now I had two counters—the counter against the front wall of the store was mine also. It included eight-by-ten silver frames of movie stars' photographs but was mostly the garden shop. I liked caring for the plants and interacting with the people who bought them. Mrs. Seay, head of the Farmers' Curb Market at the courthouse, came by often to see what I had. One day I showed her a sample of vitamin B1 that had been included in a shipment.

"What's this for?" I asked.

"It's nothing less than a miracle! Water your plants with it and stand back! They'll grow like mad. And dying ones will revive."

And they did. I could hear them growing. I had bought a sickly caladium to take home. It not only revived but flourished on B1.

I loved the roses. I studied their pictures and their fascinating names, and almost memorized the growing instructions. My favorite was the Étoile de Hollande; it was such a dark red that it was almost black. I was in my element when I helped a woman choose sixteen roses and twenty-three packages of bulbs for her yard, $6.30 in all.

A favorite gardening customer was a handsome man with a mustache and a missing left arm. He made me laugh when he said, "I buy your seeds. I plant them just as the packets instruct. I wait. But the rain comes and washes them away. Or the frost freezes them. What's left the chipmunks eat. I'm ready to quit trying."

"But you mustn't," I said. "Those chipmunks would be too disappointed. And the birds too. They love fresh flower seeds."

"The birds eat their share all right," he said. He usually ended up buying more seeds, ready to try again. I admired his voice and the educated way he pronounced his words.

I learned about plants I'd never heard of. A man from out in the country was shocked that I didn't know what a tuberose was. "You've not seen tuberoses? They're sure pretty and smell real sweet. I'll bring you some when they bloom in June." He was right—their fragrance was so strong and sweet that I smelled him coming before I saw him when he returned in June. I put the bouquet in a glass jar at the gardening counter for my customers to enjoy and wished that I had some tubers to sell too.

Sometimes at store closing time when I was making the plants neat and refilling vacancies, I found empty dahlia boxes. That was puzzling because the boxes had directions essential to caring for the plants. It didn't occur to me that someone was cheating till one day when a customer handed me a dahlia box to ring up and I noticed how unusually heavy it was. Opening the box, I found it crammed with dahlia roots, not just the one root it was supposed to have. Without saying anything to the customer, who was watching, I removed all but one. I knew she was cursing herself for buying from the regular salesgirl, who knew her stock, instead of the extra salesgirl. That's what had been happening to my dahlias!

My main counter was notions, which was made up of combs, brushes, purses for women and children, eye glasses, breath mints, incense, pipes and pipe cleaners, and many other odds and ends that people might take a notion for. A most important item was the sanitary supplies that women needed. Some people were utterly chawed to buy Kotex or Modess or Kress's cheaper sanitary napkin, Sanoval. No matter the brand, the boxes were all shaped alike so that even with the box wrapped, prying eyes could recognize what a person had purchased. Some customers asked me to bag the boxes to disguise them. I felt sorry for the men who handed me notes without a word that I then read without a word before taking their money, also without a word. While I wrapped their packages, they lurked at a neighboring counter pretending they didn't have any connection to me or my counter's contents. I thanked them with an impassive face when they collected their purchases.

As I wore glasses myself, I was especially sympathetic toward customers who needed to be fitted with eyeglasses. They always told me how they broke their spectacles, how long they'd had them, and lamented their loss. Some of them insisted that I try on their glasses—I politely resisted—to show me "how good you can see out of them." They gave me advice about mine ("Your specs are all wrong for you, you ought to have a pair like mine for nearsighted people"). One woman confided, "I had the best pair of glasses once and lost them. Why, I could even see a chigger with 'em!" Being from the country myself, I well knew how important seeing a chigger was!

Oscar Smith, our burly and gruff Brookwood neighbor, came in for me to fit him. He was pleased with how well he could read from the printed test sheet I kept beside the spectacles, and he admired himself in my hand mirror before paying me. A while after he left, I noticed an odor, which I traced to the glasses area. There I discovered his well-aged pipe stuffed with tobacco. I took it between finger and thumb to the lost and found at the back of the store where Mr. Skelton was standing.

He got one whiff of the pipe and said, "You can't put that thing in lost and found. It would stink up the place."

I took it back to notions, wrapped it well, and kept it until Mr. Smith's wife came to claim it. Her coming made the pipe episode worthwhile because she was Miss Alice, one of my favorite people. During the hardest years of our growing up she had been a true friend to us. She was the neighbor who had taken Jane and Francys to her house for Christmas.

Our fifty-cent glasses were plastic-rimmed, and the twenty-five-cent ones metal-framed. On a typical Saturday we sold at least twenty-two pairs of the fifty-centers and many more pairs of the twenty-five-centers.

I looked forward to the times Dr. Harvey Searcy himself came in to check over the glasses. "I see no sense in people who just need magnification buying expensive glasses," he'd say. "These cheaper ones do just as well."

He and I worked together: he tested his patients' eyes in his office on Sixth Street, and if they only needed magnification, he wrote down the number of the strength needed on a slip of paper, and the customer brought the paper to me.

Dr. Searcy and I both remembered that long summer he brought me through the infection that blinded my right eye when I was thirteen. We'd had no car then at the height of the Depression, and my father and I had hitchhiked sometimes twice a week to Dr. Searcy's office in Tuscaloosa where he tried everything he could think of to help me. He could not save my sight, but he kept my eye from being disfigured except for a white scar.

Miss Thompson had the main notions counter next to mine: buttons, sewing thread, cotton and wool knitting thread, and much else. Her friend, Mrs. Bowers, invited us to come to her house for lunch every day (twenty-five cents for a meat, three vegetables, iced tea, and a dessert). Unlike Woolworth, our biggest competitor, Kress didn't have a lunch counter so this offer appealed to me. The home-cooked food was tasty but walking the ten blocks to the Bowers' house and the ten blocks back in our hour lunch break wore me out. Mrs. Bowers sat at the table with me while I ate. I thought she was being sociable, but later I found out she was critiquing my eating habits. Miss Thompson said to me, "Mrs. Bowers says you eat all of one food before going on to the next food. Why don't you eat a little of one, and then a little of the others?" I didn't see what difference it made as long as I enjoyed the way I ate so I didn't change.

This was one more example of something I'd become aware of: others wanting to change me. They wanted me to fix my hair differently, to wear more makeup, and, especially, to go out on dates. Sometimes Jane and I went out with two brothers from a farm down in Bibb County. Our parents had known their parents for years, but Jane and I didn't meet the boys till they came to our work places to see us. When they visited us at Brookwood on Sunday afternoons, we drove to Lock Fourteen on the Black Warrior River to pick huge wild violets that we called rooster heads—we prized those we found with one dark purple petal—or went to the show in Tuscaloosa.

Our family sometimes visited their beautiful farm, fishing in their lake, eating fried chicken, and enjoying watermelon chilled in the spring. On one occasion Walter led us on a tour of the log house he was building. He seemed serious about Jane but Rufus and I were not serious. Rufus had brought me a bag of wild chestnuts which we enjoyed; by this time chestnuts were hard to find because of the blight. I appreciated that he had beaten off the sharp-stickered hull, leaving the shiny brown nuts that were sweetly delicious.

For one of my dates with Rufus, my feet had toughened up enough to wear my aristocrats for the first time. I still contrasted them with my clodhoppers, dubbing the two pairs "caviar and corn pone." Nobody else noticed what I had on my feet but I felt elegant.

My occasional dates with a country boy like Rufus weren't enough for Miss Thompson and her fiancé, Bill. They prevailed on me to go to wrestling matches with their friend Jack on Wednesday nights. Wrestling was deadly boring and neither Jack nor I had much to say to each other. I would have rather been at home reading one of the Pocket Books, which were new on the stationery counter for twenty-five cents. How I loved them! Of course there was not the same aura about them as a book from Lustig's but at least I could afford a couple occasionally. A most fascinating book that I chose was one to improve my vocabulary in thirty days. I kept it handy in my purse along with a novel, *The Constant Nymph*. None of the titles on our stationery counter were "dime store bodice rippers" despite what some people claimed.

To me, life was exciting enough without boyfriends. I could now afford to buy white hyacinth bulbs and a green bowl for Buddy and me to plant them in, replace the measly twenty-five-watt bulb in the upstairs ceiling light with a seventy-five watter—what a difference that made!—and splurge on a good toothbrush (twenty-five cents) for me.

These new additions to my life delighted me but Miss Thompson wasn't satisfied. She pushed me to get out and learn about Life with a capital L. Besides Jack and the wrestling matches, she and Bill dragged me to a carnival, bought me a ticket, and shoved me into a sideshow featuring something called a hermaphrodite so I would be educated about men and women. I stood with the women spectators who were crowded on one side of the sheet that separated us from the men standing on the other side. A pale person stood on stage explaining how he/she was both male and female, and pointed out the feeble little organs to edify the gapers. All I could think about as I listened to the monotone spiel was what a pitiful way to live Life!

Lately, I had become aware of coins now that I was in charge of a register. One Tuesday night my pay envelope contained a coin that I could hardly identify as a fifty-cent piece. It was burned, blistered, and battered, and I had no idea where it came from because I hadn't seen it in my register. I could discern horses on it but nothing else. I asked Miss O'Quinn about it.

"It's supposed to be a Stone Mountain half dollar," she said, "with General Lee and General Jackson and their horses. This one's probably counterfeit but we get good ones sometimes."

"I never saw one before. Will you put them in my pay envelope?"

She didn't forget. Eventually I had twenty-one of those beautiful coins minted in 1925. And I kept that terribly disfigured first one still wondering what had happened to it.

Two-dollar bills were uncommon, too, but they didn't interest me except for one thing.

"Why are the corners always torn off two-dollar bills?" I asked Miss O'Quinn.

"To cancel the bad luck they bring."

"Why, just to have a two-dollar bill would be good luck enough" was my verdict.

―――――

Constantly in the back of my mind was the terrible knowledge of war beginning. At the time, I did not fault Mr. Chamberlin for his "appeasement" policy. Daddy's brother Joe, who sailed for Waterman Steamship in Mobile, wrote us of what he saw in his travels. England had had a whole generation of young men killed and maimed in the 1914–18 war, he reminded us, and their country was not yet recovered economically. Often we listened to the radio speeches, hearing words

```
XxidxyxKx

Sunday Morning
September 3, 1939

What tragedy! Word came this morning that Britian has declared that
a state of war exists between England and Germany. If by 5 o'clock
(their time, I suppose) Germany has not withdrawn her troops from
Poland,Britian will actually declare war. Prime Minister Chamberlian's
announcement of Britian's decision (I m imajine how reluctantly he
made it) came over the air by transcription a few minutes ago. To us
who heard his masterful speech during the Czech crisis the change
was amazing. Then he was calm, confident, his voice steady and quiet.
This morning the Prime Minister's voice was heavy with sorrow and his
quiet words seemed touched with tears now and then.

Berlin is on the radio now--we hear mention of the Western Front,
the Maginot Line, Lord Admiralty etc. "It is impossible to believe
that we are having another world war."

To think that we'll never n know gay Vienna or romantic Paris or
foggy London as the young people of the past have known them. They're
almost deserted now and sandbags are piled in the streets. It is awful
to think of all war means..terror, death, uncertianty, the passing
away of all things dear and familiar.
```

Diary entry as World War II begins in Europe.

already familiar to us from our history books: the Western Front, the
Maginot Line, Lord Admiralty.

On one of these nights as we rode home on the bus, Mr. Hitt, our
driver, told us of a man he knew in Tuscaloosa: "He said he's not going to get mixed up in no war even if they invade the United States.
'But,' this man says, 'the minute one of 'em sets foot on this side of
the Warrior River, I'm gonna get my gun and kill me a bunch of 'em.'"

Tuscaloosa changed when school opened that fall in 1939. More
and more students were coming from other parts of the country for
the cheap tuition at the university. The harsh accents that grated
on my ears were made worse by the complaints of store customers
against "those damn tokens." Ten tokens cost one penny, we had to
charge one token in sales tax for every dime the customer spent, and
tax money had to be kept separate from sales money. Tokens certainly
complicated life for the salesgirl.

Male students liked to show off their smarts or maybe confound us
clerks. They would buy a chamber pot in hardware, fill it with water,
then buy several pretty goldfish to put in it, and carry the pot around
the store threatening to swallow the fish.

One student, lurking at notions, asked me for an elliptical button. I told him we had none, though I had no idea what that word meant. After he left, I asked the manager who didn't know either. He went to stationery for a dictionary.

"Oval," he came back and told me.

"Like a football," I said and picked up a card of "elliptical" buttons in back of the display. "These have been here so long without selling. I missed my chance."

We both knew the student was pranking but he added to my vocabulary.

In the new store I, who had never used a telephone before, had to get used to using the in-house phone. The store was so large and phones were so convenient and speedy that everybody welcomed them. Except me. I can't explain my terror of the phone, and I was just beginning to adjust one Saturday night as Halloween approached when the phone behind the jewelry counter rang. The store had closed, and I was busy on my counter and paid no attention until the jewelry clerk called, "Miss Kilgore, Miss Thompson wants you on the phone."

Miss Thompson's voice said, "Come to the basement. I need your help."

I flitted down to the enormous basement, shadowed and spooky with shelves reaching to the ceiling, and found Miss Thompson waiting.

"I want you to help me take some pictures upstairs," she said.

The faintest suspicion crept into my mind then. She was so independent that she would have toted those heavy framed pictures upstairs herself even if they broke her back. But I trustingly followed her down the aisle, farther and farther, spookier and spookier, till suddenly she stopped in midsentence and shrieked, "OOoooohhhh, look!!"

Her trembling finger pointed toward the dimness at the end of the aisle where I saw peering around a bin and grinning at me an evil horned devil face. I heard its teeth gnashing!

Flinging up my arms, I screamed and fled. I had no idea where I was going but I was getting as far away from That Thing as I could.

Then Miss Thompson screamed and came after me.

That Thing chased after us but had taken off its face to show it was only Mr. Thomas, the stock boy.

Then Miss Pridmore came from behind a bin doubled over with laughter. The four of us stood there, panting and laughing. Miss Thompson said, "I knew what was going to happen, but when you yelled it scared me and I ran too."

I had run so fast that I almost ran out of my clodhoppers. It was a good thing I didn't because my stockings, as usual, were a disgrace, with no feet left, only holes held together with threads.

Friday the thirteenth in October 1939 brought no particular bad luck but the day before was filled with mishaps. First, a woman looking at watchbands on the jewelry counter accused the clerk of stealing her watch. The clerk denied she'd even touched the watch. Before that could be cleared up a man appeared at the notions counter to say, "I bought a five-cent card of buttons this morning. I paid the clerk with a fifty-cent piece. I've got the buttons all right but I just realized she gave me change for a dollar." He couldn't remember who had waited on him. Miss O'Quinn came to check the register. Yes—it came up fifty cents short. Now we were all under suspicion.

Then the salesgirl in hardware laid a twenty-dollar bill on the register while she recorded the sale. Wind blew in the open door, caught up the bill, and tumbled it down the trash chute to the basement.

"You should have seen the trash flying while we searched for that twenty-dollar bill," Miss Hamner told us later. "No question—we had to find it."

One day I was back on Miss Johnson's counter just as she was selling a large picture I especially fancied, a clipper ship. I smiled at the buyer and said, "You're buying my picture."

"Oh, I don't want the picture," she said. "I just want the frame. Let's take the picture out."

We tried to remove the small nails from the back of the picture using pliers but couldn't get them loose without damaging the frame.

"That's all right," the woman said. "I come in often. I'll bring the picture back to you."

I thanked her but discounted what she said. I knew people were busy and forgot promises. But some days later, when I got together all the photos of movie stars I'd saved from the picture frames I'd sold and took them to Miss Burns, she showed me all the pictures she had collected from the large picture frames she'd sold. There was my swift-sailing clipper ship! I bleated "That's mine!" and grabbed it. Miss Johnson, standing nearby, said, "Yes, a woman brought it in and said to be sure and give it to you. But I forgot." I was glad to get it and pleased that the customer remembered.

Daddy was on jury duty again for a week ($3.00 a day) so I commuted with him for free and used my bus ticket money to renew my subscription to *Life* magazine. Then he was called to work in Hybart in Monroe County, Alabama. He arrived there on the 4:00 A.M. train, slept till 7:00 A.M. on a cot in the office, and went to work at 8:00 A.M. Besides the depot, there was only one store in Hybart, a honky-tonk, a cotton gin, and a small house. The trees hung with long gray moss and a big swamp stretched under the trestle. Daddy suspected it was inhabited by alligators. He wrote that the mosquitoes were as big as grasshoppers. The storekeeper invited Daddy to go with him to Camden in Wilcox County. "As we passed the courthouse in Camden I saw Governor Miller in his law office," he wrote Francys at Livingston. "He still uses oil lamps." I felt a kinship with the frugal governor because when we had no money to buy gas to run our Delco we had to revert to coal oil lamps too.

Jane and I were becoming disenchanted with riding the bus from home to work and back. Every night we had to wait at the station for two hours before we could get a bus home. That wasn't too bad when one of us had to work late or when there was an error in my register. In the latter case, I and every salesgirl who had used my register that day would have to stay after the store closed for register school: each of us had to recite the proper order of ringing up a sale to Miss Hamner before we could leave work. That seldom happened, however, and Jane and I were doomed to two hours of waiting in that horror of a bus station.

As I sat still on one of the hard benches, I could watch the big rats creeping around searching the floor for food. The walls of the women's restroom were peppered with peep holes (sometimes you could spot a fried-egg eye watching you). Messages, vulgar and otherwise, were written everywhere. And the whole place stunk.

To occupy the time, I had bought knitting needles and a how-to book from Kress, and we set ourselves to learn knitting. That undertaking was not too successful as far as I was concerned. My neck scarf of Kelly green was a project with no ending—it grew longer and longer because I was stuck on the purling page.

Jane and I discussed moving to town. "Think of the time we'd save," I marveled. "What we could do!" Furthermore, Jane had several boyfriends who didn't have cars so living in town would aid her social life.

Mama undertook the search for a suitable room, accompanied by Mary Alice who enjoyed seeing inside city houses. A house with a big veranda on Main Street across from Miss Thompson's place pleased both of them. Mama made an appointment with the brother and sister who owned the house for Jane and me to come see the room. I learned with concern that their name was Harris. I knew a Mr. Harris as a picky and contrary customer. Even with these reservations, Jane and I on our lunch hour went to the appointment. We liked the looks of the house and, after all, we wouldn't have to see much of our landlords. We rang the doorbell and waited. And waited. We rang again, longer. And waited, longer and longer. No sound in the house at all. We couldn't believe they wouldn't keep their promise. We knocked and knocked. Nobody. We finally turned away, realizing they must have peeped at us and not liked what they saw. We did not suspect what a blessing this was to prove for us.

Mama and Mary Alice renewed the search and found us a reasonably priced room in a gray cottage on Sixth Street. We wouldn't have far to walk to work, Miss Thompson was only a block away, and there was a small restaurant on the corner between us, Jesse's Café. Moving in was simple as the room was furnished.

CHAPTER FOUR

TOWN LIVING INTRODUCED US TO a new way of life, a life so full of comforts and pleasures my Baptist soul felt guilty. Getting used to the gas heater was hard—I was sure it would explode or poison us as we slept. But oh, that heat on cold mornings was nice! And having a functional bathroom with hot water for a bath! We were used to taking "bird baths" with a wash pan and cold water, except on Sunday nights when we bathed one after the other in the washtub by the kitchen fire.

The most wonderful thing about our new life was our landlady, Mrs. Davis. She would invite us into her room to listen to the University of Alabama football games and to *Major Bowes Amateur Hour* and other popular programs on her radio. But after I discovered her stack of magazines, I spent my time looking at them. She also would treat us to delicious sweets from her kitchen like homemade brownies and mincemeat cookies with a pecan in the middle. What joy one night when we came home from work late and found two small custard pies sprinkled with nutmeg waiting. I went into a swoon as I ate mine— that smooth vanilla custard was so delicious.

We ate sparingly at Jesse's Café except for Thanksgiving in 1939 when late in the day the turkey dinner was reduced in price. The waiters, Rudolph and Edgar, brothers attending the university, told us, "Choose any amount you want—five cents' worth, ten cents', whatever." We ordered a dime's worth of turkey and dressing for each of us. The plates arrived overflowing with tender turkey, cornbread dressing, giblet gravy, candied sweet potatoes, green beans, and ambrosia, all for a dime. What a feast! I told Jane it was the first time my stomach was filled up since we left home. Usually we supplemented eating at Jesse's with cold meat, rolls, baked sweet potatoes, and parched peanuts that Mama and Daddy brought us from home.

With Christmas approaching, Kress was so busy that I couldn't keep up with the date. But I always knew how many shopping days were left till Christmas because hanging on the mirror at my counter was a calendar. Every night before leaving work, I tore off the current day's notice to reveal how many shopping days remained. At "Seven shopping days before . . . ," Miss Thompson was filling a special order for Partlow State School, an institution for intellectually disabled young people, Miss Powell had left for lunch, and I had both notions counters plus the counter across the front of the store. At "Three Shopping Days Before . . . ," we sold twenty-three sixty-cent purses and twenty-four fifty-cent ones! We were so busy I hardly had time to breathe.

At McLellan's, Jane returned from lunch one day just in time to see a man slip four pairs of her most expensive stockings inside his shirt, Christmas presents for the women in his life perhaps. When he saw her coming, he fled out the side door into the middle of the bored Fitts Taxi drivers waiting for a call. As soon as they saw Jane running after the man, they took up the chase and caught him. They extracted the stockings from his shirt and returned them to Jane who stood to lose several dollars off her counter profits. But the pilferer, a Black man, paid more dearly—the judge fined him ninety dollars and sentenced him to ninety days in jail, which seemed excessive to us.

Jane had always been popular with girls as well as boys. In high school, she was chosen Miss Citizenship and several times Miss Brookwood for her beauty. Her thick dark-brown hair curled naturally, and she had dimples and an endearing attitude of kindness toward everyone. I had not noticed that she favored any one of her many boyfriends more than the others until a fellow named James kept coming in to see her at the store, asking for a pair of socks for a one-legged man, his way of joking and trying to get Jane's attention. Before long James began walking her to our room from work, sometimes stopping in at Baker's Café. What concerned me was how closemouthed Jane was about their relationship. What little I knew I found out by accident when Miss Ewing (toy counter) let it slip at lunch that she and Jane were double-dating with James and his friend Square. This relationship with James seemed to be different from any of Jane's other boyfriends, but I couldn't understand what the difference meant.

An interesting diversion came my way one night during a lull in customers. I asked a man who was studying over our tobacco pipes if I could help him. His answer tickled me: "No, I'm just gaping." We began talking about pipes and he pulled one out of his pocket.

"I bet you've never seen one of these."

I hadn't.

"It's a Meerschaum," he said. "I got it in Germany in 1923." He handed it across the counter for me to hold.

I had read about such pipes. I inspected it with interest. The bowl was like yellow ivory and the stem was bound on by copper wire.

"Foam from the Black Sea washes up on the rocks and dries. After hundreds of years it has petrified and can be cut into these pipes."

"It must have cost a lot more than my pipes," I said.

"Thirty-five dollars."

Later I told our assistant manager, Mr. May, about the Meerschaum because I knew he had a pipe collection.

"I don't have a Meerschaum," he said. "But after work on Saturday nights I get out my Chinese pipe. It's made of clay and the stem is twenty-one inches long. I smoke it in bed while I catch up on the week's newspapers."

I smiled to myself picturing tall, lean Mr. May in his PJs sitting among his pillows surrounded by newspapers and smoking that long clay pipe. In my thoughts I put a nightcap on his head.

On Saturday December 23 we were so harried and busy that we did many senseless things. Miss Ryan made three register errors by just not thinking. Miss Powell and I did worse. We sold purses to two women at the same time. My customer gave me even change. Miss Powell owed her customer fifty cents change. While I was registering, Miss Powell gave my customer her customer's purse and fifty cents change and the customer disappeared. I was left with my customer's purse and no change for Miss Powell's customer. After we got that settled to the woman's satisfaction, I strode up to another woman who was looking at hair-straightening combs, and blurted out "Thank you!" instead of the usual "May I help you?" She looked startled and hurried away.

As we parted that night, Miss Thompson gave me a gold locket with a fancy "A" engraved on it. I requested a picture of her to put in it. My gift to her was house slippers and a hound dog statue.

I walked home alone and staggered into our room at midnight. A great comfort was the box of assorted homemade cookies Mrs. Davis had waiting. I ate several to gather strength to make myself ready for bed. Jane came in a bit later having walked home in James's company.

The next day, Jane and I gifted Daddy with a Baby Ben clock, small enough in size for him to transport easily and an accurate timekeeper for his work as a telegrapher on the railroad. We wanted to give Mama a corset, but she requested the money to pick it out herself. I gave Mary Alice money to choose a sweater, and we bought lipstick and powder for Francys.

Between Christmas and New Years at the store, we were not very busy with customers but worked hard changing counters back to the way they were before and papering the spaces (that is, putting fresh white paper on the display shelves).

On New Year's Day, our family ate generous portions of the good luck foods: hog jowl, collards, and black-eyed peas. Buddy had chicken pox, a light case. Daddy was driving the car to work at Freight Yard Junction in Birmingham.

Jane and I were glad to have Christmas and inventorying behind us. Taking inventory was especially hard: we had to count every item in our understock, every item on the counter, and every item in our stock upstairs. Jane's was even more complicated than mine. She worked so late into the night that she went home with Frances Meigs, another salesgirl whose father was a jailer. The family lived in the solid, square old jail with the prisoners. Jane said there were lots of noises in the night. Mama was delighted to shock Francys by writing her, "Jane spent last night in jail." But then she explained why it happened.

After Christmas, when we returned to our room in town, we took a gray-striped half-grown kitty named Mickey to Mr. Woods at his little grocery store across the street from the bus station. We so hated to give away any of our cats, believing that nobody would love them as much as we did, but our feline population was constantly growing— we had to get rid of some of them. We left Mickey with Mr. Woods and went on to work.

That night after store closing, as Jane and I shivered through the cold dark toward Jesse's and a hot supper, we found a gray tabby kitty sitting on the post office steps.

"Mickey?" I called, unbelieving. "Mickey!"

He came to me meowing, "Home folks! At last!"

It wasn't possible. How had a cat off the farm for the first time safely crossed that wide, busy Greensboro Avenue to Brown's crowded corner, walked the long block past Woolworth Five and Dime, crossed the avenue from City National Bank, and gotten past Kress to the post office? That was the way I walked to work. Could he track me? How did he know to wait on those steps for us to come? I picked him up and held him close under my jacket for warmth. His purring vibrated against my heart.

Jane and I stood there. What to do? The night was too cold to walk back to Mr. Woods's with him. If we could get him to our room at Mrs. Davis's we'd keep him inside. But where could he stay while we ate supper? We decided to leave him outside the café and hope he'd wait for us.

When we told Jesse our problem, he said, "I been wanting a cat. Give him to me." We brought Mickey inside and left him in the warm kitchen with the cook who set down a saucer of chicken for him. The next day the cook told us, "That tomcat worked all night. He caught so many rats he couldn't eat them all. I had to throw them in the slop bucket."

The first Sunday of 1940 Jane and I stayed in town instead of going home. We went wild, spending a total of $1.60. Snoozing in bed till eleven eliminated the need for breakfast. We proceeded to Pickles Café for a midday dinner of plump oysters, crisply fried outside and moist inside, accompanied by a form of cornbread new to us, hush puppies. Then it was on to the movie theater beside the Tuscaloosa skyscraper to see *Ninotchka* with Greta Garbo. What a delight, how we laughed. Garbo's accent charmed me and we thought her beautiful.

On January 12 after store closing, our family went to tour the new county agent's office with the rest of the farmers and have refreshments. Coffee and every kind of cake imaginable were spread out on the table: several versions of pound cake, chocolate cakes frosted and unfrosted, caramel cakes with nuts pressed in the top, lemon bars—there I stopped because I came to the homemade doughnuts. I had heard of doughnuts but I'd never seen one. Wonderful! I even wrapped a doughnut in a napkin and slipped it in my pocket when I thought no one was looking.

Buddy, not over his chicken pox yet, was much aggrieved when he realized I hadn't given him a Christmas present. I explained that he got so many other gifts that I thought I'd wait and give him something to wear. In his eyes "something to wear" wasn't a gift.

In mid-January the weather turned very, very cold—sleet, ice, and snow. The frigid wind was so strong on January 19 that Daddy couldn't drive the sixty miles home from Birmingham in our Model A. In its worn-out condition, its peak speed was about thirty miles an hour. With no hot bricks to put at his feet, he would have frozen. Mama kept Buddy out of school, the first day he'd missed, but that long walk in such weather for a little boy just getting over the chicken pox wouldn't do. Mama quilted and sewed dresses while keeping the fire going and listening to firecracker-like explosions in the house—pipes freezing and bursting. Snow was already six inches deep and mounting. She kept the chickens fastened in the chicken house with servings of cornbread in warm milk. The cows and calves she kept in the barn with extra portions of sweet feed.

At the store, customers were so few that Mr. Skelton said I could have the next day off. I asked for an additional day, packed my nightgown, and with Jane trudged through the cutting wind, ice, snow, and dark to the bus station. The streets were unlighted and there was no traffic. I could hardly stay on my feet; the sidewalk was so slippery and my leather-soled shoes provided no traction. But I was on my way to Brookwood, which was motivation to endure almost anything.

At the bus station, Bill Martin, another Brookwooder, popped up from reclining on a hard-worn bench and said, "Where do you think you're going?"

"Home" was my confident reply, not reading the signs all around me—no passengers lining up, no drivers evident, the one bus parked in the drive fastened tight and glistening with frozen snow over its top.

"How're you going?" he asked. "All buses are cancelled."

The ticket agent verified his statement. Nothing to do but go out in the slippery dark again and return to Sixth Street. The snow reached above our oxfords and soaked into our shoes. By the time we got safely inside again, I was trembling with the cold.

Since I was marooned, I spent the time writing letters. In one to Francys at Livingston, I included two dollars, but later as the severe weather continued I wrote a postscript: "I was sending you two dollars but now the snow is so deep I'll have to buy galoshes with one of the dollars. I'll send it to you later."

Wearing my new galoshes, I went on a shopping spree; I bought a rose-colored suede cloth dress with leather belt and buttons at J. C. Penney's for three dollars and paid down on a black and white one at Louis Wiesel's for four dollars. One was a size eleven, the other size thirteen, but both fit fine. While out in the weather, I went by to see Jane at McLellan's and sat with her while she ate lunch, and then to Kress to meet Miss Thompson and lunch with her at Baker's Café. Stores had few customers and the clerks were pranking and partying.

For January 29, 1940, all of our family was home. Francys's friend, Nolen, was just home from navy boot camp at Great Lakes and joined us wearing his sprucy uniform. Two other fellows appeared during the afternoon, and my sisters went off with the three of them to the show. In February, the weather settled down to rain, business picked up, and life's routine in town returned to normal.

Jane and I arrived at Jesse's for supper one night wringing wet because we forgot to take our umbrella to work. Rain still poured down when we'd finished eating.

"Jesse's coming soon," Edgar said. "I'll take you home in his car if you can wait."

Before turning the car over to us, Jesse did something under the

*Aileen splurged
and bought this
dress, which she
often wore to work.*
(The University of
Alabama Libraries
Special Collections)

hood and it started right away. The fun ride home was cancelled by
the car refusing to start after we got out. Fetching our umbrella from
the house, I held it over Edgar while he struck matches trying to figure out what Jesse did under the hood to make the car go. Jane managed the steering wheel and the choke at Edgar's directions. The car
wouldn't budge. The rain poured down so hard on the umbrella that I
couldn't understand anything Edgar said.

Finally he gave up. Taking the umbrella, he walked back to get
Jesse. Jane and I were inside drying off when Edgar, soaking wet,
returned the umbrella and drove the car away still in pouring rain.
What price chivalry! I had hoped that one of the brothers and Jane
would get interested in each other. The boys worked hard at the café,
kept up their studies in law school, and seemed to be steady fellows.

I was concerned about the James situation; he and Jane were seeing each other so often that I was worried. He came across to me as a fly-by-night kind of person; from some of my past reading the word "gat-less" came to mind to describe his footloose and fancy-free character, but only to myself. I did not speak of my doubts to anyone. I only observed. One night we were in bed ready to turn out the lamp when he came knocking on our door. Jane got up, dressed, and they took off for parts unknown.

Miss Thompson bought a new chair for her room and gave the old one to me. It was overstuffed and very comfortable. I was glad to have it but there was a transportation problem. How to get it across Main Street and down the avenue to our room? Finally we just picked it up, Miss Thompson on one side and me on the other, and lugged it to Mrs. Davis's. We squeezed it through our narrow door and rearranged the furniture to fit it in.

On Sundays Jane and I sometimes walked to Calvary Baptist Church with Mrs. Davis. She was like a tour guide pointing out interesting places along the way and telling us about the families she knew. And what a world of difference between the worship service there and what we were used to in the country! I especially enjoyed the music. The Sunday school superintendent turned out to be one of my customers, and I noticed many of my artificial flowers decorating hats.

Tickets went on sale March 20, 1940, for the long-anticipated *Gone with the Wind* movie. Jane and I shared the cost of tickets for the rest of the family for the afternoon of March 28. They had to be home before dark to do the night chores. Jane and I planned to go see it after work the same night.

At the last minute, Daddy came in the store to tell me he couldn't use his ticket because the railroad had called him to work. I was so regretful, but I knew how much the work meant to Daddy's self-respect and pocketbook. I just wished he could share this experience with the family. We had no difficulty turning in his ticket.

What excitement to be a part of the crowd streaming into the theater that Thursday night. I lost myself in the beauty of the film, not suspecting what misery it would later cause me, even almost getting me fired from Kress. I thought it excellent "but not as wonderfully told as the book," as I wrote in my diary. Clark Gable didn't strike me as a sincere Rhett. He looked the part all right but I didn't like his acting of it. (Nobody else agreed with me!) Vivien Leigh was lovely. I couldn't find any fault with her Scarlett.

The Saturday before Easter we were run ragged, selling ninety-seven women's purses and thirty twenty-five-cent children's purses. Most of them were the dark winter purses. How relieved we were not to be stuck with them now that the white ones were available. We sold out of Easter lilies. Usually I never heard how much my register took in, but for this Saturday before Easter Sunday, my register alone took in $2,200.

That night I crept into our room on Sixth Street at eleven and collapsed. So tired, so tired. I had bought a dress for Mama that day for an Easter gift as she had refused to buy one for herself. I knew she would complain about its cost but she might wear it after all.

April 15 all the Kress salesgirls had to work late counting the slow sellers, items on display and in the stock room that weren't justifying the space they occupied. When only Miss Thompson and I were left on the Floor, hungry and tired, she asked Harry who was passing by with trash bags, "Where's Mr. Skelton?"

"He went down to the basement."

She galloped over to the candy counter, gathered a handful of my favorite (and the most expensive) bridge mix, brought it back to notions, and we were rejuvenated. I thought of some saying I'd read, surely not in the Bible: "Stolen tidbits are the sweetest." This was a serious transgression and we could have been fired if we'd been caught. Harry was so honest it never occurred to us that he would participate.

One morning Mr. Skelton, without a word, handed me a letter from a woman in Fayette, Alabama. She wrote, "I bought a purse on March 28th. I paid the girl fifty-one cents for it. On returning home I found a receipt for twenty-five cents in the sack. I plan to be back in Tuscaloosa on the first Friday in May and I expect a refund."

Of course, this reflected on me, but I trusted completely the salesgirls who worked with me. I didn't worry that any of us cheated her. I was concerned that there'd been a mix-up in the receipts, but each receipt had the register number where it was sold. Mine where the purses were was number fifteen. As I never saw the woman and never heard another word about this problem, it must have been easily settled.

Later in April 1940, through the glass front door near my counter, I watched the 4-H students straggle past the store toward the flagpole, running to keep up in their parade. Years rolled back and I saw myself in Armistice Day parades—gawky, cold, and hungry. In other words, countrified, the epithet those of us who came from the sticks most hated. The way we talked, the way we dressed, the way we acted, revealed us as a *homo rusticus*, a term I remembered with a grin from our literature book.

That same day the *Gone with the Wind*–style snoods arrived and to my horror were unloaded on my counter. Word came that each clerk should wear one of these crocheted bags to hold her hair at the back of her neck. I hadn't ordered the monstrosities so I refused, but my extra salesgirl had to wear one. Snoods looked glamorous on Scarlett O'Hara in the movie but not on us ordinary women. Nobody had enough hair to fill up a snood; each hung limp like an empty fish net. The colors weren't even pretty.

Then came the day when Mr. Skelton gave me an ultimatum— wear a snood or be fired. That was no choice—I couldn't give up my job. Every salesgirl in the store had to tie on a snood and did we look bedraggled. I didn't see why anybody would buy a snood after seeing how awful they looked on us. You wouldn't have mistaken any of us for a character in *Gone with the Wind*. The atmosphere in the store was not one of happiness. But I was astonished—immediately the awful things began selling. The first day that everyone wore a snood I sold seventy-seven! At that rate I hoped we'd soon sell out. Then I discovered the total snood order was for ninety-two dozen. Endless and hopeless.

Two customers who came in the store often were both elderly but opposites in other ways. One, very wrinkled, rouged and lipsticked, always wore her fur coat no matter the season. When she stopped at a counter, if the clerk didn't get to her right away, she'd clack a coin against the glass, calling out in her raspy voice, "Girlie, will you wait on me, please?" Everybody in the store would look to see who the negligent clerk was. If I happened to be seated out of sight on the low stool I used to check the understock for what I'd need tomorrow, that clacking coin and croaking voice would chill my blood. I'd throw down the order pad and spring to her command, red-faced and feeling as guilty as I looked. And I hated to be called "girlie."

The other customer's face was clean of makeup except for powder. Her clothes were neatly ironed and she always wore a hat. Her face would light with a smile if I'd gotten in a new shipment of boutonnieres. She bought the flowers to pin on her dresses and hats. Over the bridge of her nose was always a bandage. With time the bandage grew larger and yet larger. She never spoke, but she looked at me across that bandage with eyes that longed to tell me things. I didn't know what to say to her except the usual "May I help you?" Then I'd count out her change and say "Thank you" with sincerity.

One Sunday afternoon as Jane and I sat in the porch swing with Mrs. Davis, she reported that two men involved in the oil business had rented her back apartment. "The older man is engaged," she said. "Here he comes now. Looks like he's been golfing." He rested his golf clubs in a rocking chair while she introduced us. As we were chatting, the younger man, Mr. Frost, came onto the porch and lingered with us while the other man went inside. Mr. Frost was much younger with a round face and a pleasant manner. After that, he began taking Jane out sometimes. She also continued to date a fellow named Pete when we were in the country. Pete worked for Joe Avery, the same businessman in Howton that Nolen had hauled coal for. Mr. Avery rented several farms about the county to raise feed for the mules that worked in his mines and on the farms.

I wrote Francys an account of the Sunday afternoon Mary Alice and I were invited to take a drive with Jane and Pete in his boss's new car: "We'd drive along for thirty minutes in silence then Pete would say, 'That's our company's field out there.' Five minutes passed with Mary Alice and me on the back seat straining our ears to hear. Jane eventually said, 'It is.' After driving another mile or two Pete would say, 'That's our farm over there.' After a few minutes of looking Jane would agree, 'It is.' That's the way conversation went through Brookwood, Abernant, back to Rock Castle, and home again."

Suddenly, I became aware that James was not coming to see Jane anymore. She made no comment to me but she began going out often with a brakeman on the Alabama Great Southern Railroad. She wrote Francys that he was "very nice." He drove a Plymouth automobile, and I liked him too. I wrote in my diary: "He's very gallant, not simperingly so but just as though it's expected of him. His name is Clarence."

At this time, Mama was taking the 1940 census, going from house to house to list the residents. She was having a hard time, especially in the Lock Seventeen area on the Black Warrior River between Tuscaloosa and Birmingham, "the wildest place in Alabama" according to my reading. "Just writing a note as I don't have time to even turn around," she wrote Francys. "My job is a JOB—I neither sleep nor eat and am always tired. That's from driving over such ruff and rocky roads."

Many moonshiners lived in those hills and hollows. They came up out of the woods, Mama said, red-faced and smelling of wood smoke, sour mash, and sweat. While she filled out their forms, they spat snuff or tobacco juice through a crack in the floor. One time a sixteen-year-old boy had to answer Mama's questions for his parents, and some adults had to sign their name with an "X." I was surprised that none of them balked at answering the census questions.

Mama commented on their use of the English language. Many of their words she recognized from when she was growing up in Pickens County, where old-time expressions were still in use. At one home place, a man splitting stove wood complained to her, "This here axe is dull as a froe." A froe was a tool similar to a pick except not sharp, Mama explained to us. Another man told Mama he couldn't take time with her right then—he was on his way "to chunk those dad-ratted hogs outta the peanut patch." He meant to throw rocks at the pigs. And a woman told Mama that she had spent the morning "tolling her hogs home with a bucket of shorts"—luring them with wheat feed. I knew from my hog-slopping days that shorts were a favorite of pigs, but I never knew before that they were also a favorite ingredient of the moonshiner's product. At one house, the woman asked Mama if she would "back" a letter she had written to her daughter in West Virginia. Mama figured out that she meant address the envelope. The woman knew the address by heart and watched carefully as Mama wrote it. "My daughter's backslid since she went up there," the woman lamented. "She's taken up drinking and smoking too."

At a lonely shotgun house without even a hound dog in the yard, Mama fell through a rotted yard gate. Fortunately, she was able to pick herself and her portfolio up and stagger to the porch to recover. It turned out that an elderly widow lived there alone. She didn't even have a glass of water to offer Mama.

I did not tell any of these stories at the store. I did not want the backwoods people laughed at. However, Miss Thompson and I came in close contact with just the opposite kind of person because of a lost dog. I noticed a pocket-size bull dog wandering about in the store and pointed him out to Miss Thompson. "I believe he's lost," I said. "He's been here all day and no human has shown any interest in him."

Our lost and found was at a desk in the back of the store, the same place I initially took Mr. Smith's pipe, and we didn't customarily deal with animals. But this little fellow clearly needed help. Miss Thompson telephoned the number on his collar. The person who answered was grateful but couldn't come for him right away. Harry took the dog to the basement for safekeeping.

When the woman came to claim him, she was beautifully dressed and talked the way rich people in the movies did. She tried to pay Miss Thompson for calling her. "I'm grateful you've taken such good care of Disraeli," she said. Miss Thompson refused the offered tip, which worked out to my advantage because the woman then went to Lustig's and bought a box of elegant candy that I had longed for when I went there with Daddy. She then left it with a note of thanks at the back desk for Miss Thompson. We shared the candy with Harry, though I noticed he took only one piece. The chocolates were even tastier than I had imagined all those months ago.

On May 15, 1940, I heard the newsboys in the streets shouting an extra. Though my counter was near the door, I couldn't make out what they were saying. Harry was outside washing windows. When he came in, with fearful heart I asked him what had happened.

"The Germans broke the Maginot Line," he said.

"But I thought it was unbreakable," I lamented, not realizing that though this line of fortifications might have saved France in an earlier time, now we were dealing with a different kind of Germany: a grim, unstoppable military machine. Unbelieving, I tried to put the news out of my mind, but that wasn't possible as most customers came in with a pink extra folded under their arm, headlines black across the top.

———

In family news, James was back even more often than before. He took Jane to see *Rebecca* and she gave him her picture. She wrote Francys in Livingston: "I have only one beau now and that's James. I gave up Clarence, and Jack Frost moved away. I gave Pete the go-by. I haven't heard from J.L. in a long time. But I'm supposed to have a date with Bill Higgs some Sat. noon."

I didn't envy my sisters their complicated love lives. For me, it was ideal to be able to join in their social activities without having to suffer the tangles of romance. I didn't want a future where I was tied down young as a wife and mother. I wanted to get an education and see the world. One day through the bus window I saw a girl I'd known in school in a yard we passed. Her wedding had been the day before, I knew, and here she was on her honeymoon morning scrubbing clothes on a washboard in her mother-in-law's yard, with a fire going under a big iron wash pot where they boiled the clothes. I did not want that future.

As James came so frequently, I was surprised that Jane agreed with me that we should move back home in order to save money for a new car. We had to face the fact that our family's Model A was not safe to drive. Its shaking seizures had become so violent that the car was uncontrollable. On our way down River Hill with Daddy to get an ice cream treat at Pure Process, it shimmied and wobbled so wildly that I thought surely we'd end up in the river. On other days it wouldn't start, and if Daddy was gone, Mama had to send for Shag Rollins, who lived just below us near our peanut patch. He could work magic on old, worn-out cars. But sometimes even Shag couldn't handle our Ford.

Before we could take action on our decision, I ended up in the hospital with appendicitis, or so Dr. Shamblin diagnosed. His bill was one hundred dollars. Five other Brookwooders were in the hospital ward where I was—six hundred dollars from Brookwood alone. I wondered about that but the pain was real enough.

There were ten of us in the ward, and much joking and gossip went on despite dreadful abdominal cramps the nurse told us were caused by the ether and unavoidable. I felt blown up to the bursting point with no escape valve for whatever was inflating me.

One of the other patients was Freda from Mrs. Wilson's seventh grade. I hadn't seen her since then, but I well remembered that whenever an unsatisfactory school day was drawing to a close, or a storm was battering our school windowpanes, Mrs. Wilson called on Freda and her twin to sing for us. Back then Mrs. Wilson had overruled honky-tonk tunes such as "She Had the Habit of Giving Everything Away," which most of us knew unbeknownst to our parents. Now our hospital ward echoed with those forbidden honky-tonk songs—"I don't want yore greenback dollar / I don't want yore diamond ring / All I want is yore heart darlin' / won't you take me back ag'an"—and hymns led by Freda. Just as the singing of the twins had uncurled the kinks of those unhappy seventh grade days and sent us home content, so our singing in the hospital made us all feel better.

Not until a week after the surgery did the doctor allow me to get out of bed into a wheelchair. On the eighth day he told me I could walk. Two weeks after the operation, he had the bandages removed and said I could go home but not go back to work until four weeks postsurgery. Four weeks out of work and a bill for $100 to pay with my weekly pay, which was $9.80 for six days work.

During my recuperation at home, I spent time listening to short-wave radio broadcasts from London. The certain doom of the British Expeditionary Force at Dunkirk was a monstrous black cloud hanging over us all. What would the United States do if Britain fell? It seemed impossible that the trapped soldiers could escape total destruction. When we heard that an impromptu fleet of workboats, sailboats, and worn-out old vessels was heading for France to rescue an entire army, we didn't see how they could succeed.

But they did.

Some of the most moving programs were broadcast after the spectacular rescue. I wrote in my diary: "I heard an Englishman read a poem about British ships from way back in time up to Dunkerque. He said he'd never forget 1914 when those long, grey battleships slid like ghosts out of the mists of the sea, recalled from all over the world to defend England. At last he came to the little pleasure steamers that usually carried the crowds on excursions in the evening and on Sunday, but were used on that fateful summer day to rescue the British Expeditionary Force from Dunkerque. The *Gracie Fields* was one he knew well. She made trips to Wright Island and back and many's the time he went along. 'We used to laugh at them,' he said, 'but we shan't laugh anymore . . . not after Dunkerque. They made an excursion to hell and came back gloriously—but not the *Gracie Fields*.'"

Gracie rescued over one thousand men from the beach before she was sunk by German aircraft.

CHAPTER FIVE

BY AUGUST 1940, MANY RECRUITERS for the different branches of the military were seen about town, very eye-catching in their uniforms. The Tuscaloosa National Guard was ordered on maneuvers. Most of the local boys were included. Miss Hamner's brother, who worked in the shoe store next to Kress, had to go. She asked him about the rumor that they'd be gone for a year. He finally said it was true. "My mama would have nine puppy dogs with crocheted tails if she knew that," Miss Hamner said—a painfully vivid figure of speech, but a situation many women faced.

The constant wail of the phonograph provided the background for everything we did at Kress but the theme changed now from hillbilly heartthrob songs to "I'll be back in a year, little darlin', Uncle Sam has called and I must go." Time passed. That record sold and the next song faced reality: "He's 1-A in the Army and he's A-1 in my heart. He's gone to help the country that helped him to get a start." Everyone was realizing we were in for the long haul.

A young man who had been coming in for some time to buy my hand mirrors always beamed at me. One day as I gave him his package of mirrors, I said, "What do you do with so many mirrors?"

"I put them in the ladies' room at my place—seems like they get broken or folks take them home." He looked at me with his frank, shining eyes. "Whenever you go out dancing how about coming to my place?"

"Where is your place?" I asked, not mentioning that Baptists were not dancers.

"It's Dick's, in the forks of the Birmingham Highway and the Keene's Mill Road. Our fried catfish is the best, right out of the river."

I thought a minute, then I knew—that old sharecropper house set in thick trees and bushes, with cars parked around it at night. When we passed it, I would strain my eyes to see what was going on inside but it was always too dimly lit. Dick's smiling open expression didn't match his place of business.

Jane and James were making plans to take the Greyhound bus to Livingston to see Francys. Then Mary Alice who had been sick for several days complicated our lives by ending up in the hospital. Dr. Shamblin diagnosed appendicitis but kept her in the hospital for observation. He decided she might not have trouble again for ten years and sent her home. I thought what really held him back was the ninety dollars I still owed him on my appendectomy.

Unfortunately, Mary Alice's many beaus knew where Jane and I worked. They popped in at all hours inquiring about her and interfering with business. While she was recuperating at home, two of them came calling on the same night. The one who had to leave first because of a work commitment let the air out of all four of the other fellow's tires.

Fortunately for many reasons, Mary Alice never had a recurrence of the appendicitis problem (if that's what it was). Mary Alice's romantic adventures kept us entertained partly because we knew those high schoolers involved were too young and footloose to be considering anything as binding as marriage. Like Jane, Mary Alice attracted the fellows' eyes wherever she went.

In one of Mary Alice's letters to Francys she wrote: "We had a fight in the classroom Friday. We were having literature when it started. John T. was looking on my book and Alton shook my desk a little and John T. could not read so he told Alton to quit. But Alton shook it again and laughed. John T. jumped up and started beating on him. They had to go to the office. Alton told the principal it wouldn't have been John T.'s business if he shook me out on the floor. . . . Got a pretty Valentine from Commer. He put his address on the envelope so I guess I will have to write him and say I got it."

Not long afterward, John T., who came from that wild Lock

Seventeen area Mama dealt with during her census days, was summoned to the office for misbehaving on the playground. The principal, busy with paperwork, tried to reason with John T. about proper behavior. John T. heard none of it. He suddenly grabbed a baseball bat leaning against a chair and attacked the unprepared principal. John T. not only bloodied the man's head but knocked out two of his teeth and broke his arm before help came. We felt that Mary Alice and Alton got off easy in their problem with John T.

That summer we had such a blooming of all kinds of flowers. They popped up everywhere, and some of them we had not seen in years. The Cape Jasmine bushes (gardenias to city people) in particular were loaded with the white satin-petaled flowers that were so intoxicatingly fragrant. One Saturday night we brought Luna, a neighbor, home to Brookwood and delivered her to her door at about eleven o'clock. It was a night when the moonlight was so golden bright that it made the air feel heavy. In the middle of Luna's yard stood a Cape Jasmine bush nearly as large as a haystack and covered with blossoms.

"Oh, I wish I had a bouquet," Jane said.

"Get out right now," Luna said, "and pick you as many as you want." Which Jane did.

Sitting in the car near midnight with that lemon-sweet fragrance wafting in the window, I watched my sister, drenched in moonlight, picking those luminous flowers. I could not understand the strange feeling that came over me. I only knew that I was watching a moment to be remembered, a moment when the world paused before making an irrevocable turn.

Back in the everyday world of Kress, we had a spate of stealing by small boys. The tobacco pipes on my counter especially attracted them. I was busy with a customer one day but keeping my eye sharp on two boys who appeared to be brothers. When they hurriedly headed for the street door and I saw a pipe missing, I left my customer and ran after them. I caught them half a block away at Liggett's Drugstore. Yes, the older one had the pipe. I let the younger one go (he was about Buddy's age) and turned the other one over to the stock boys in the basement.

Later one of them paused at my counter as he went out to lunch. "That boy's been caught stealing before. But I think we cured him this time. We scared the living daylights outta him." After the boy was let go, the basement had to be scrubbed, I heard, as they had scared more than the daylights out of him. Then Miss Falls caught a boy stealing from the toy counter. It was his first offense, at least at our store. The stock boys put him to work helping them and made him sweat.

Fall brought an influx of business from rural families because of harvested crops and the cotton being sold. One day a little girl stood at my counter hugging a brand-new fifteen-cent doll while her mother selected a comb.

"What's your dollie's name?" I asked.

The girl was about five, roly-poly with platinum hair and a cupid's smile, but too shy to answer.

Her mother looked down at her and said, "Tell her how you picked cotton to buy your doll."

I grinned at her with understanding. I never got a doll out of the cotton patch though I did once get a pair of shoes.

We were impressed that Daddy worked at Jasper in September 1940 when President Roosevelt came to Senator Bankhead's funeral. The President's Special stopped right outside Daddy's office window, so he had a good view of everything. He told us the first news we had that the president couldn't walk. His attendants had to set him in a wheelchair.

The Secret Service was strict with Daddy the day of the funeral—they wouldn't allow him to give out any information over the phone and they watched his every move. Afterward Henry Wallace's car drove up to the depot, and a man came in to buy the secretary of agriculture a ticket. To come home, Daddy rode to Birmingham on the Congressional Special, the train that had brought Bankhead's body to Jasper. In the car, he found Bankhead's burial permit, made out with place of death, cause of death, and so on, and signed by his doctor, and handed it over to the conductor. When he finally reached home, Daddy was worn out.

I enjoyed hearing what Daddy told of events he saw in his work, whether of national importance like Bankhead's funeral or of the daily life of ordinary people. Once Daddy rode what was known as the "colored excursion train" from Winfield to Birmingham. The passengers were in high spirits. When the train pulled into the Birmingham station, a woman passenger leaned out the window and hollered to a sharp-dressed man, "Come here, baby. I know the good Lord opened up those pearly gates and you got out." What a fancy way to call somebody an angel, I thought!

One September night in 1940 Harry, as usual, waited at the door to lock it after me.

"Miss Kilgore, have you heard the good news?"

I hesitated. The latest good news I'd heard was that Mr. May, our floorwalker, had given a big diamond ring to Miss Quinn, a clerk at Jane's store. Miss Quinn was tall and slim, as was Mr. May, and her pretty face was made even prettier by the generous sprinkling of freckles over it. Jane and I liked her very much. But I didn't think that Harry meant news like this.

"No, what?"

"You, Miss Goins, and me, we're getting a raise."

This was a surprise because I hadn't been at Kress very long, but that didn't dim my gladness. Eleven dollars a week now. I felt that I'd come up in the world.

Miss Thompson came home with us on Saturday to stay until Sunday afternoon. Every time we were with her she had a new date for her and Bill's wedding. Now she said "after Christmas." She rode back to town with Jane and Clarence—yes, he was back—as they went to the show.

Jane's trip with James to see Francys never happened. Now Jane and Clarence were planning to go see her. I had given up trying to figure out what was going on. Clarence gave her a pretty compact and two pairs of sheer hose. The latter was an iffy matter as only "fast" girls accepted gifts of apparel from men. But she was also seeing Richard whom I hadn't met. He'd joined the air corps and would be leaving soon for three years. She went to the movie *Wyoming* with him.

Meanwhile, life went on for our family in spite of social life complications and the constant threat of war. Daddy was working at Yale Yard, an important railroad yard in Memphis. Buddy was pale and sick, with the hard measles this time. He had a Lifebuoy chart that he was supposed to mark when he washed his face, brushed his teeth, and shampooed, but I caught him scrubbing his face with a dry washrag. He liked for me to read stories about Beowulf to him, especially the part where Grendel came up from the bottom of the lake and slew the Viking warriors asleep in the castle. Mama was canning for winter, and all the women were doing a lot of quilting, preparing winter bedcovers. And every year around Thanksgiving, women of our church made a quilt for the Baptist Orphans Home in Troy. They quilted with tiny neat stitches that were very artistic.

As Jane and I worked six days a week and were gone from home from 7:15 A.M. till 9:00 P.M., seldom did we go to church because of washing, ironing, mending, and other things that had to be done on Sunday to prepare for the coming week. But usually something entertaining was happening at one or the other of the churches, especially the "other" one that was Little Hurricane Baptist. I still belonged with Mama and Daddy to staid old Big Hurricane Baptist, which dated back to 1838 when a group of settlers, including Native Americans and a Black couple, built a plain square house of worship in an extensive longleaf pine forest near Big Hurricane Creek. My sisters had joined Little Hurricane where there were more young people and an energetic leader for them.

But Little Hurricane always seemed to be in turmoil over something. At a church conference Brother Collyer got up and said, "There's somebody in this church telling tales. They're going around saying that Preacher Riley is bringing base women down from Bessemer and taking them swimming in the gravel pit. The next person telling such a tale, I'm gonna take them directly to jail."

Now Preacher Riley, pastor of the church, was an upright great-grandfather a bit bent out of shape by a lifetime of farming. I was glad I wasn't present; I would have giggled, but the men were dead serious.

Brother Joe stood up and said, "Why take them to jail? Why not make them stand up and say they told it?" He sat down.

Silence reigned while everyone kept still.

Then Brother Hogg stood. "I told Brother Collyer," he confessed. "But Brother Otha told me."

Brother Otha jumped up. "I told Brother Hogg but Brother Vassar told me."

Before he could sit down Brother Vassar was on his feet. "I told Brother Otha but Brother Dorr told me."

Brother Dorr was absent so the inquiry stopped there, except for Brother Joe's closing statement: "Nobody who had any sense would credit such a tale. Bessemer has a whole lot more to offer a base woman than we do, and who would come way down here just to swim in a gravel pit?"

When my sisters regaled us with this story, Mama's comment was succinct: "And men claim that women gossip!"

Brother Collyer seemed impelled to keep things in a threatening stir. When he and another brother disagreed in Sunday school class on the age of the earth as set forth in Genesis, Brother Collyer, with a flash movement, drew a knife. Brother Crabtree succeeded in bringing him to his senses but it was a worrisome incident. At a later conference, when the members were considering a list of twenty names up for censure, Brother Collyer's was the first name to be considered, but not because of his temper. The complaint against him was he attended church and took part in its decisions as if he were a member. But he had never put his letter in the church so he was not a member. The church voted to withdraw from him. In a temper Brother Collyer declared he would never bring his letter to turn it in to the church. "I'll show all of you. I'll start my own church and I'll steal every member you've got in this blankety-blank church, and where will you be then?" And he stalked out and started his own church the next Sunday, but it never seemed to damage Little Hurricane's membership in any way.

In contrast our church, Big Hurricane, was abuzz over Brother Pintegar's Bible teaching. He stated that anyone who killed an ox was a murderer the same as if he'd killed a man. Mrs. Hogue's jaw dropped and her eyes bulged. She turned to Mama to say, "Well, law, plenty of folks do it." But Brother Pintegar went on to explain that the difference was whether he butchered the ox for food or killed it in a passion of anger. A sigh of relief swept over his listeners. Oxen were so slow and patient that they seldom spurred any Big Hurricanite to a passion of anger.

But it did bring to Brother Wallace's mind the time he returned from a trip to Tuscaloosa and left his ox team yoked outside his front porch while he took a load of groceries to the kitchen. Twilight was coming, he said, and he lingered too long getting a drink of water in the house and chatting. Then desperate echoing bellows brought him running to his team. A large black bear was attacking the yoked oxen as they stomped and bellowed and butted. He managed to drive the bear away with a heavy shovel he kept in his wagon for emergencies. "And that," Brother Wallace added, "was a mere thirty years ago. Who knows what might be in our woods now?"

Of more concern to us at the moment were the human thieves lurking in the woods. On one Saturday night alone, someone stole all of the Marshes' chickens at Howton then went a few miles back of them and stole all of the Pruitts' chickens and turkeys. "The thieves cleaned them out," Mama said. "I wouldn't be surprised to wake up some morning and find all of ours gone." We trusted our dog Jack to warn us, but he wasn't always at home as he did wander on some nights.

I had to leave worries about chicken thieves to Jack and Mama because things were changing at Kress. Why did I not wonder at the reason I was taken off my counter and put in charge of Miss Thompson's? The news that she was leaving Kress startled me; she had finally admitted that she and Bill had married two months before in Mississippi. In talking with me, she had postponed their wedding date so often, and made such a big to-do about it, that I took for granted that it was far in the future and so I had nothing to worry about. But now she had to quit work because Kress employed only single women. I was bereft to lose her. Like Harry, she had been a rock of dependability for me but there was no going back. I faced the intricacies of her counter, the main notions counter, which was far more complicated than my own, with a word from my twenty-five-cent vocabulary book: trepidation.

The wool and cotton yarn was the most intimidating. When a customer began a large project, she had to make sure she'd have enough thread of the same dye lot to complete it because dye lots varied. So the understock was crowded with boxes labeled with names, and the women came in and bought yarn as they needed it. Complicating matters, Mr. Skelton then informed me that, due to supply uncertainty given the world situation, we had to order enough yarn to last a year—that was beyond me. I was grateful that he was patient and helped me.

The buttons were difficult too. I had to make sure I had every button displayed, but there were so many of them. And I never realized there were such varied colors in sewing thread. We carried two brands: the old one, Coats, and a newer one that we were pushing probably because we made a bigger profit. But women kept coming in complaining how the new brand knotted while they were trying to sew with it. They stuck with the old J. & P. Coats. And oh, those new-fangled zippers! We had a brand of our own that we pushed, but women were always bringing back malfunctioning zippers and demanding the national brand. Then there were shelves I had to keep decorated attractively to catch the eyes of the many women who crocheted, knitted, embroidered, and tatted. We also had two new types of looms that necessitated I learn how to use them and make a sample rug from each one.

Difficult indeed.

Over all of our daily life hung the imminence of war. In the summer of 1940 changes in Tuscaloosa became more personal to me. Mr. Thomas, the stock boy, was called up; Miss Hall left for a better-paying job; Miss Yow, Miss Armand, and Miss Cottingham, all regular salesgirls, married.

On a broader scale, Royal Air Force cadets from Great Britain began training at Hargrove Van de Graaff Field in Tuscaloosa. Their instructors came from other parts of the country and brought their families with them. The RAF cadets came in the store almost every Saturday night in groups, always high spirited, ready to stir up excitement. One night, word flew over the store that a bunch of them announced to a clerk that the United States had added a fourteenth stripe to its flag—a yellow stripe—because we were too cowardly to join Great Britain in the war. Most of us were too busy to pay attention to their hijinks.

One afternoon I noticed a tall young man at the crockery counter. I knew that Miss Pridmore was off for lunch and nobody else seemed to notice him. As soon as I could leave my counter, I went to help him. I recognized his light blue shirt and navy trousers as the uniform of a flight instructor for the RAF. He spoke in a rather flat voice and seemed very quiet in manner. The most striking thing about him was his eyes—a deep blue bordered with dark lashes. He knew exactly what he wanted: a plate, a cup, a saucer, a glass, and a knife, fork, and spoon. I wrapped them, handed the package to him, accepted his pay with thanks then returned to notions. But I didn't forget those blue eyes.

A victim of rumors was the slight young Japanese American man who performed wonders with yo-yos. A crowd always gathered round him back near the toy counter, and yo-yo after yo-yo sold to bedazzled customers. I enjoyed the show he put on, but all I knew was that he came out of the New York headquarters. Soon word went around that he was a Japanese spy, and we didn't see him anymore.

A National Guard unit from the New York area, returning from maneuvers in Louisiana, camped at the armory just east of Tuscaloosa on the Birmingham highway. Most of them came into Kress that Saturday night, and they were not in good shape or good humor. Some had an arm in a sling, others were on crutches, all of them were scratching and cursing chiggers, ticks, ants, mosquitoes, and the South in general.

"Those damn crocodiles," one said to me. "Their tails were like iron, they'd take a swipe at you, immobilize you, then eat you alive."

"You mean an alligator, don't you?" I said.

"Alligator, crocodile, there's no damn difference. The whole South ought to be cut off from the United States and sunk into the Gulf of Mexico."

"And good riddance!" agreed another.

They seemed to want to express their sufferings more than to buy anything so I said nothing more.

These National Guardsmen were passing through, but other strangers to the South were sent to live here for the duration. Two of the women became very important to me. Plump, blonde, and jolly Mrs. Garl was the wife of a flight instructor stationed at Van de Graaff Field. I stored many boxes of thread for the tablecloths and bedspreads she was making. We always had an interesting chat when she came in.

One day when I came home, Mary Alice met me with the news that a training plane from Van de Graaff Field had crashed at the spring where we went for our water. She saw it fall and was among the first to reach the scene.

"The plane was a mess, smashed into the big trees, tore off a wing. A broke-off tail," she told me. "The cadet was sitting against a tree—somebody was wiping blood off his face. A couple of men pulled the instructor out of the wreck and laid him on the ground. He was real still, pale, but I didn't see any blood." She took a deep breath. "But he opened his eyes—they were the prettiest blue I ever saw. He sort of shuddered and Mr. Gibbons said, 'He's a goner.' Somebody spread a handkerchief over his face—his blue eyes were still open."

I knew.

The next time I saw Mrs. Garl I mentioned that the plane crashed near my house.

"Yes," she said, "That was Carl Knauer. A good boy. Far from home." She stood silent, looking down at the colorful skeins of thread on my counter. "Those British cadets are reckless and without fear. Every time an instructor gets in a plane with one of them he's at risk."

Mrs. Garl lived in Buena Vista, the same new subdivision as my other favorite new customer, Mrs. Huffman. Her husband had to do with forestry. She was tall, well-educated, and well-spoken. She kept busy knitting and crocheting for the baby she was expecting. As the summer grew hotter and more humid, and she grew bigger and more awkward, I noticed how she seemed to be suffering. The last time she came for thread, her eyes, in her brown-splotched face, looked painfully distressed. When I didn't see her for a while I thought nothing of it, so when Mrs. Garl came in the store and told me Mrs. Huffman had died giving birth to an eleven-pound boy, I was unprepared. Her body was shipped home to Ohio for burial. I found the short notice of her death in the newspaper and kept it.

Not long afterward, Mrs. Garl again came in, this time to tell me goodbye; she was going back up north. Her husband had asked for a divorce after falling in love with a local girl who worked at the airport. "There's absolutely no chance for a reconciliation," she said.

I grieved for both my customers and sadly took their yarn out of storage to make it available to others.

I was deeply grieved also to see in the newspaper an account of the killing of Lois Williamson, another of my customers, by her ex-husband. He stood in the dark on the street below her upstairs apartment and shot her through a window, then killed himself. I had often seen Lois at Perry Creamery, where she worked, when I went there for chocolate milk, and she had been in our store earlier the night of the tragedy. I was realizing more and more that allowing myself to care about my customers was exacting a price.

The British cadets, whom we came to know through Mary Alice and her friend Jessie, were brashly unlike the Southern boys we knew. We discovered, to our embarrassment, some words that were ordinary to us had a different and shady meaning to them. One cadet, Derek, sang a song praying for unlimited beer for the airmen, a regiment of sons for the queen, and other things we thought not appropriate to pray for, all in language he warned us never to use. Once when we commented unfavorably on a girl who was skimpily dressed, Derek said, "You have to display your goods to sell them." Sell your goods? What was he talking about?

At least their sense of humor was like ours—they loved a Pocket Book I had bought from the store which was a collection of comical mistakes that students had made on exams and homework. When the cadets came to our house, they always grabbed that paperback and sat reading aloud from it and guffawing. One example of misspeak they repeated over and over had to do with the definition of a virgin forest: an expanse of trees where the hand of man had never set foot.

As Christmas 1940 approached, all cadets were confined to the airfield. The ones we knew refused to accept the discipline—they escaped, climbing a high fence in the night. Derek and the others went straight to Birmingham, they told us later, in search of women and alcohol. But Ronnie, our favorite, came to Brookwood where we made him a part of our quieter celebration.

As a result of this escapade, they were all told they'd be sent back to Britain to be reassigned. Downhearted? Not at all. Here was another adventure to be wildly experienced. They were eager to wade into it. "Derek will of a certain be allowed to fly again," Ronnie said. "He's too good. But for the rest of us, I don't know." Mary Alice and Jessie saw them off at the AGS train station in Tuscaloosa. The cadets kept up their laughter to the end.

Sometime later we saw a small notice in the newspaper: a British transport ship, returning from the United States, was torpedoed and sunk by a U-boat just off the coast of Britain. Over five hundred RAF trainees were lost. We wondered, but never knew.

Derek had taught me Cole Porter's "Begin the Beguine" which I loved: "Let them begin the beguine, make them play, till the stars that were there before return above you."

Though our friends from the other side of the world were gone, my dime store life was still full of interest. Often McDade, a Greyhound driver from Mississippi, was at the station when Jane and I got there after work. The three of us passed the time walking around town together. Once we found Santa Claus at the toy shop almost swamped by a crowd of children. We laughed to watch him try to pose for charming pictures with each one. Some smiled willingly, but others squalled with fright or tried to jerk his beard off. He had developed an unobtrusive but powerful arm hold for the uncooperative ones. It was easy to see why he was sweating.

All of the family except Daddy got home by eleven thirty Christmas Eve night. The house smelled so good—apples, oranges, the Christmas tree. Buddy had told Mama that if Santa had come when we got there to be sure and wake him up. Santa had come all right but she didn't wake him. Buddy had written a note with help: "Dear Santa. Here is some cake for you." An arrow pointed to a white saucer with two slices of fruit cake. Before we all got in bed he woke up, and every five minutes from then till daylight he said, "Is it time?" "Reckon has he come yet, Mama?" "Can I get up?"

Finally, at daylight Mama allowed him to get up and did he "oh" and "ah" over the electric train Daddy had helped choose. I could hear him from upstairs even with my head under a pillow. Mama called

*Mary Alice (left)
and her friend Jessie
Gerk see Royal Air
Force cadets Ronnie
Gilbert (left) and
Derek Berry off at
the Alabama Great
Southern depot in
Tuscaloosa.*

from her bed, "Buddy, put your clothes on before you start playing," for the house was very cold. In about half an hour, she went in the living room and found him, naked as a jaybird and covered with goose pimples, choo-chooing the toy train and dressing himself at the same time. Mama said later that she wouldn't have gotten up when she did but she hated for him to discover Christmas by himself. The rest of us were unable to stir. The aches in every joint and soreness in every muscle brought to my dim mind the old saying "I feel so bad I'm just not worth killing."

Daddy missed all this for he was in Pensacola, Florida, then Dora, Alabama, followed by Sumiton, Alabama. He hadn't heard a word from home for several weeks and got so worried about us that he sent a telegram to Jane at McLellan's.

I was too weary to write him but not too weary to eat pieces of the four cakes—pineapple, lemon, and two kinds of fruit cake—Mama had made plus baked chicken, cranberries, cornbread dressing with just the right amount of onion and sage, and potato salad. Adding to our joy was the unexpected arrival of Miss Alice, wife of Oscar Smith of the stinking pipe episode and daughter of Old Man Bill Prude, who joined us at the table.

By late January 1941, Daddy had worked a week at Potts Camp and then was sent to Tupelo. He wrote Francys at Livingston: "I don't know when I will get to go home. . . . Guess I will have to hang in there and keep up with my work, however I do get so tired of running around and working all times of day and night."

We remembered his birthday, January 22. Jane sent him two shirts and I planned to give him a pipe. I knew he would be thinking of his little sister Nettie who had his same birthday. They had celebrated together with the cake their mother made for them until Nettie died at age three.

By this time, I had come to an appreciation of how differently Clarence treated me from the way James did. I was shut out entirely from Jane and James's relationship whereas I often rode home with Clarence and Jane. On one of these nights, as Clarence and I waited for Jane to get off from work, he pulled out a small square box, flipped it open to show me an engagement ring and wedding band, both set with many stones.

"I'm popping the question to her tonight," he said with delight.

I did not voice my doubts but this seemed premature to me. It turned out that she refused him, and they agreed not to see each other for a month. But within a week he showed up after work to take us home.

I realized he meant to persist until she did say yes.

February 1941, Daddy and Sid were putting up fences, getting ready for the new Stock Law to go into effect. All farm animals would have to be confined now. I was glad. Before this law, getting rustled or hit on the highway was a constant danger for livestock. That, or being so starved when the first green of spring showed, a desperate animal ate poisonous plants that kept it from finding its way home. Twice in the past, neighbors had sent us word that a calf of ours was down

Aileen with her favorite calf, Skinny Dugan, and the chicken house in background.

and couldn't get up. Once was at Mrs. Wallace's spring; that was John Buddy. Mama dosed him on alum water, forcing it down him with a syringe. Another day Mrs. Stevens sent us word that my pet, beautiful Skinny Dugan, was dying at her water hole. We brewed gallons of coffee and forced it down the almost-gone Skinny. And how I prayed over her as dark came on. I wanted to spend the night with her but, as Mama pointed out, I had to catch the 7:15 bus for work the next morning. All that day I was in suspense. When we got home that late afternoon, there was Skinny looking over the fence as I walked up the lane. I cried with relief. With this new law, our animals would no longer be in danger.

On January 27, 1941, Buddy wrote to Francys at Livingston College:

Hello Guffy Socks
I have a YO-YO.
It is red and black.
And I can YO-YO it good.
Bring me something when you come home.
Bring me some Saf T pops when you come home.
Love Buddy

The last week of February we had snow, sleet, and rain every day. Francys came home for the weekend anyway but fell sick. For her return, Mama and Daddy took her to Tuscaloosa to catch the bus back to Livingston so she wouldn't have to stand on the side of the road to wait for it, but Daddy still worried about her. On the way out of town, he stopped at a phone to call the bus station to check on her. The bus for Livingston had left, so he knew she was safely on her way.

Riding the bus regularly as we did, Jane and I got to know the drivers. I was astonished at how unkind some of them could be to the Black passengers. When the bus I was waiting for came in from Meridian, passengers going beyond Tuscaloosa got off to walk around. A nice-looking young man who was laughing and talking with the other passengers while waiting to re-board caught my attention.

Meanwhile the driver checked all seats for order, collecting forgotten packages and trash. In the young man's seat he found a billfold. A card inside with a photograph identified him as "Negro." The driver waited until all passengers had reassembled for boarding, with the young man standing in the center of the group.

The driver said to him in a distinct voice, "Have you lost anything?"

The man looked puzzled and searched his pockets. The driver held up the billfold, and the young man happily identified it.

But the driver said, "You're sitting in the wrong section of the bus, aren't you? Negros sit in the back of the bus."

I never saw happiness so quickly and completely damped down as I did then. Without a word the young man accepted his billfold and went to the back of the bus. I thought this was cruel.

When I boarded the bus one morning, McDade, the Mississippi driver, looked me over and said, "What's the matter with your hair? Why haven't you combed it today?" Well, I had combed it to no avail; it was just too skimpy and thin. I looked into his laughing eyes and said solemnly, "It's the cooties. There are so many I can't comb it." Before he could react, I was moving down the aisle searching for a seat and Jane had stepped up and handed him her ticket.

I didn't realize that passengers who heard what I said to him would not want me to sit by them. Purses, books, and packages suddenly occupied the vacant seats. I couldn't find a place till I got to the back section labeled "Colored," but I was well entertained there. I listened to an elderly preacher talking nonstop to a pretty teenager. He quoted to her poetry he had composed: "My love for you will truly flow, like water down a cotton row." I knew well the joyous feeling of watching rain fall on a cotton field after a drought. I enjoyed listening to him more than the teenager did, I thought.

McDade often told us of his misadventures. He said he was minding his own business as he sped down the highway in Number 442 when a bee flew in the open window. "The blame thing landed on my head, I let go the steering wheel just for half a second to beat it off. The bus went wild every which way knocking down a coupla mailboxes. I left 'em pretty flat. And just my luck, one of those checkers that floats around spying on us reported me."

We laughed at his discomfort but we laughed harder in a grim way at what Rufus, my farmer friend, had reported to me the previous Sunday: A girl living near his farm missed her school bus one morning. Her boyfriend missed his WPA work truck. There they stood on the side of the road with nothing to do. They decided to hitch a ride to Mississippi where there was no waiting period and get married. "She had a good enough home," Rufus added. "Now it's going to be root, hog, or die for both of them."

Daddy wrote Francys that he left home for Birmingham on the 8:00 P.M. bus March 13, took the train to New Albany, Mississippi, arriving there at 5:00 A.M., and began work at 8:00 A.M. He was working first trick: "I'm a little tired tonight. . . . That was good on your grades." By March 24 he was in Dora, Alabama, with Memphis, Tennessee, scheduled next.

Jane was planning on breaking up with Clarence again. He was having a woman knit a dress for her birthday gift; that wouldn't do at all.

Mr. Skelton offered me a job in the office. I said no without hesitating. How dull life would be handling money in that upstairs office with no windows, keeping check on employees to see that they didn't make off with anything without paying for it. Working on the Floor was exhausting but interesting—you never knew who might come in, or what might happen.

One day I noticed Dr. Searcy's receptionist-nurse looking at the spectacles. I greeted her with gladness but I wasn't prepared for why she'd come. "I'm retiring from Dr. Searcy's," she said. "He sent me to ask if you'd be interested in taking my job." I felt honored. Dr. Searcy would be wonderful to work for, and I was sure I'd work only five days a week and be paid a much higher salary. But I pictured those dark rooms with their antique furniture shut away from the world down there on Sixth Street and said, "No, thanks."

The war situation was intensifying. Hordes of soldiers and sailors were on the move. Rumors said there'd be no leaves granted after June 1. Even on Sundays military convoys thundered past disturbing the peace of the rural Sabbath. The sharp-eyed and bored GIs spotted Francys at Little Hurricane Baptist teaching her Sunday school class in the shade of a tree. The soldiers yelled and waved to get her attention as they passed, but Francys never looked their way. The little girls giggled and nudged each other. "They're waving at you," they said, forgetting about Jonah in the belly of the whale on his way to save Nineveh. "You could at least wave and help the army's morale," we told her. But of course she couldn't, not after Mr. Crabtree had told Mama what beautiful church manners her daughters had.

Bus drivers told us that fifteen busloads of soldiers had passed through Birmingham one after the other destined for Louisville, Kentucky. Our nightly home-going bus, Number 442, was commandeered to haul a load of soldiers out of Hattiesburg with McDade driving. When 442 limped back from that trip it was a wreck—door handle broken off and tied back on with a string, the door itself hanging on with one hinge, gear out of socket, and stinking of beer. McDade said that at every stop the fellows bought a sack full of beers for themselves and a sack full of Co-colas for him.

One morning as I came out of the bus station to walk to Kress, a bus was backing away from the curb. Suddenly it returned to the curb, and the door screeched open to the sound of empty beer cans rolling down the aisle to the front.

"Long time no see," McDade hollered from the driver's seat. Instantly the load of soldiers was attentive, hanging their heads out the windows, looking and listening.

I stopped walking. "Where are you going?" I asked.

"Top secret," he said, grinning, but the soldiers began hollering, "Hattiesburg!" "Memphis!" "Louieville!" "New Orleens!"

It didn't matter. As far as I was concerned, any listening spy was welcome to that bunch of wild, unkempt, hungover varmints. The odor wafting out of the open door was disgusting.

"How do you stand it?" I didn't subdue my voice. "If their mamas could see them now, they wouldn't claim them."

"It gets worse," he said.

I kept walking and the bus backed up again and pulled away from the station.

On July 5, 1941, Francys's beau Nolen said goodbye after a two-week leave from the navy. He said, as we gathered on the front porch to see him off, "There's going to be war, no doubt about it."

From our house on the hill, we watched him walking on the road toward Birmingham through rain and mud in his white uniform, depending on somebody to pick him up.

I noticed that Dick's roadhouse was dark now with no cars parked around it, and I was no longer selling mirrors by the half dozen. Dick had probably been called up. I hoped with all my heart that war would not extinguish that joyful light from his eyes.

Jane and I finally bought the car, a black Chevrolet. We'd talked about it off and on for so long that it was hard to believe we'd finally acted. The last night of bus riding I was alone, sitting behind Heyward who was driving. McDade was deadheading, standing beside Heyward. There were others on the bus toward the back but no locals to stop for so we barreled along the road directly into a huge golden moon just rising. In the dark bus it was as if we three were alone. We talked about this and that, the draft, the war, what was ahead for McDade now that he was classed 1-A.

Suddenly he turned to me and said, "I know what's the matter with you."

I sighed. Even McDade wanted to reform me.

But I was mistaken.

He declared, "You're in love with me."

I was so shocked I gasped. The two of us had hardly ever said a serious word to each other. He and Jane were friends—I just tagged along and enjoyed myself. For one thing, I made fun of him for quitting college to drive a bus ("Money!" he said). But had I in any way acted "fast"? That was the worst that could be said of a girl. But I was confident that I hadn't. He and I had never been in any sort of situation or conversation that could be called flirtatious.

I stared at McDade, speechless. The relaxed tone of our being together had changed. Heyward kept silent, driving steadily on. When we came to my stop, I refused McDade's help down the step. In sweet tones I said as I passed him, "I'll be praying for . . . ," and I paused to let him think I'd say "you," then added, "the Japs and the Germans now that you're coming." And I left him without a "goodbye" or a "good luck" though I knew I would not see him again. I walked up the lane puzzled and angry, drowning in moonlight.

For a while every time he drove past our house on Sundays and at night, knowing that we would be at home, he blew the bus horn. When I didn't wake up at night hearing it, I knew he'd gone.

For Jane and me, having the car was wonderful, no worry in the morning of missing the bus, no hurry, and a relaxed drive to town. Best of all was the coming home as soon as our stores closed. Jane was a skillful driver and enjoyed it. I was content for her to take charge.

Some Sundays she drove toward town alone, smartly dressed and wearing a hat. Where she went she never said but I was convinced it was to see James. Now I began thinking about my future. If she married James as events indicated, I would not want to continue commuting by myself. I had to make plans for such a time. Whatever work I went into I wanted it to be helping people in some way. I began investigating nursing schools. Most of them, I found out, charged an entrance fee as did Druid City Hospital in Tuscaloosa. Grady Hospital in Atlanta and Charity Hospital in New Orleans did not. The Atlanta hospital invited me to a weekend when they were hosting a gathering of prospective students. I asked Mr. Skelton about giving me time off to go to Atlanta for that weekend. I told him I was thinking of leaving Kress to go into nursing school. After hemming and hawing a bit, he agreed to let me go.

The day I left, I boarded the crowded train at the Alabama Great

Southern depot before daylight. I'd never set foot on a train before. I was bug-eyed over the new experience. I knew I was well turned out: Mama had bought me a hat on sale at Rhealee's Hat Shop and remade a silky beige dress with an overblouse of beige linen. I was wearing my new watch I'd bought from Fincher and Ozment on Main Street, a Bulova with a second hand for my career as a nurse. I was that sure of my future!

At the Atlanta station, I took a taxi to go wherever the hospital was, my first ever taxi ride. The driver chatted on the way and I told him why I was there. He said the hospital was in a part of Atlanta with a high crime rate. When he stopped at the nursing school and we found the door locked, he wouldn't leave me. I rang the bell several times before I heard someone coming.

A hefty woman in a white uniform opened the door. I waved thanks to the driver, picked up my small bag (six dollars from C. W. Lewis Furniture) and followed her inside. As she walked down the hall ahead of me she said, "So you want to be a nurse." She cackled a laugh that knocked the breath out of me and froze stiff the hairs on the back of my neck. Later I could never describe it; I only knew the effect it had on me then. The sound echoing in that strange empty hall made me vow I'd never, never go into nursing.

She showed me into a large room filled with beds neatly made and pointed to one. For the rest of the weekend I went to every class, listened to all the talks, and watched the other girls who had come, but when it was over I boarded the train with a made-up mind. Nursing was no longer in my future. I still meant to change my life—I just didn't know how.

What happened on December 7, 1941, should not have surprised us after Nolen's prediction the last time he was home, but it did. That Sunday was a quiet church day. Daddy was with us and so was Francys, home from her sixty-dollars-a-month teaching job in Abernant. After midday dinner everyone except Jane took a drive to the bottomless Blue Pond at Vance, the big scary-looking crater filled with still, blue water, then on to the Cottondale Cemetery to visit the Kilgore-Morris graves.

Daddy remembered each one as we wandered among them pulling weeds and straightening tombstones. Here was Uncle Dan and there was Uncle Johnny. Both had walked home from the Civil War minus a limb. Grandpa Morris, who had been brought from England by the textile mill owner at Scottsville to take charge of all the machines, came home in 1865 to a burned mill and desolation. He opened a small shop in Cottondale where he cobbled shoes and sold candy.

Late that afternoon when we returned to our own home, our minds had to readjust from tales of that past war to word of war in our own time. Jane, white-faced and breathless, met us at the door with news of the Pearl Harbor attack. Because of immediate censorship, we didn't know the extent of the damages, but we knew this was serious world-changing business. We kept our radio on far into the night.

The day after Christmas 1941, McDade came into the store to see me. Soldiers were a common sight, but I knew who he was as soon as he came in the door of Kress. I made no effort to attract his attention, but he found me anyway reworking a counter. Discouraged and weary from the Christmas rush, I wished he hadn't found me. And when I saw how confident and fit he looked in his uniform, I was wildly jealous of the wonderful change in him. He was outgoing about his life: he was stationed at Ft. Leonard Wood in Missouri but would soon be transferred, he thought.

"It's great to get back here and see all my ole buddies, the ones who've not been called up yet," he said. I could see how red his eyes were and knew that over Christmas he'd been doing a lot of celebrating. "At the station here I found old 442," he continued. "I jumped in and took it around a couple of blocks just to make sure I remembered. It felt good to be in the driver's seat again. When this is all over, I mean to come back to Tuscaloosa, this country suits me."

"How long are you here for?" I asked.

"My furlough's about over, got to leave for camp tomorrow."

"But when are you going to Mississippi to visit with your folks, your mother?"

"I don't have time this trip. But see this money order I'm sending her?" He waved it at me.

I took a deep breath and looked at him, red eyes, handsome face, uniform and all. "If you think," I said slowly, "that money will take your place with your mother at Christmas or any time, you are stupider, dumber, and more no-count than I thought." I turned my back, shoving the blocks around to fit the counter space.

He stuck the money order in front of my face. "But look how much it's for," he said. "I've hardly spent a penny of my pay so I could save this for her. I'm on my way to the post office now to mail it."

I refused to look at it. "And you're right here in Tuscaloosa, almost to the Mississippi line," I said shaking my head in disgust.

"But I'll see her next time."

"It's late," I said. "You'd better go before the post office closes."

My last sight of him going through the door into his wide world was blurred by tears, for his mother, I thought, but later I knew also for me. When would I have the courage to make my move?

I will do something, I will change, I will, I will!

Time passed and I suddenly realized Jane was no longer seeing James. I became convinced this was final because James and his gang began coming into Kress late Saturdays when I was most tired and rushed to jeer at me. This had never happened during their several previous breakups. He had even made up a nickname for me, a name that reduced me to nothing.

"Zero is a good girl," James would say as he walked the length of my counter trailed by his shadows, chunky Square and a tall solemn fellow who wore black-rimmed glasses. "But who in the hell wants a good girl?"

He sometimes chortled, "Say, Zero. How does it feel to be a dime store floozie?" That was the first time I'd ever heard the word. What it meant I didn't know but it didn't sound complimentary.

If he caught me sweeping the floor within my counter, he made me so angry that I wanted to raise my little red broom and whack his sly grinning face with all my might. What made me control my temper? I'd be without a job in a flash.

But one Saturday he came in alone. He had no grin on his face that night. "Aileen, I hear that Jane is going to marry Clarence. Don't let her do it. He's a monster, the low-downest of the low down, not fit for her to wipe her feet on. Crud, that's all he is."

What he said was drowned out by my remembering his jeers of those past Saturday nights when I'd been Zero to him. I wanted to snarl, "It takes one to know one!" But I said nothing, just continued working and waiting on customers. Years passed before I understood what it must have cost him to humble himself to beg for Jane's safety.

Later Eva Wilson, who knew our family well and had taught every one of us in school, told Mama, "Don't let Jane marry that Clarence fellow. He's about the worst boy I ever knew. Cruel and sadistic." We'd never heard those words used about a person before.

I had seen no evidence of such traits during any time I was with Clarence. I had even been to his home to meet his hospitable mother and talk with his father, who had served in Cuba during the Spanish-American War. I felt that James and Mrs. Wilson both must be wrong and I said nothing.

But anyway, it was too late. Jane and Clarence had secretly married several months earlier in Mississippi. Marrying secretly was not like Jane. Did she suspect she'd hear things she preferred not to know? The Plymouth automobile, it turned out, was not his. It belonged to his parents. And he moved Jane into one room at his parents' house.

Despite all the family uncertainty, life on the farm continued on schedule. Daddy bought fertilizer and seed and rented Johnny Gaddy's mule to plow our field in April 1942. As he plowed, he was well entertained, as was the whole Brookwood community, by the last RAF flyer we were to know, Idwal Jones. On clear spring mornings, Idwal flew out over our house to do stunts in his training plane, loop-de-loops, upside down with wavering wings, rolling over—what a show! One day he flew away then returned with a buddy in another plane and they put on a double show for everybody.

It was through Idwal I learned about another tragedy to strike those who had immigrated to Tuscaloosa to take part in the war effort. Idwal talked often of an instructor he liked so much. "All the chaps like him. He's a jolly regular fellow." His name was George Steinwedell and he came from the Twin Cities. Idwal claimed that he took the cadets on binges and told them about the famous Hollywood people he knew, Gene Tierney for one. Steinwedell, only thirty years old, died after a three-week hospital stay. Idwal attended his funeral. "The most

Royal Air Force cadet Idwal Allen Jones with (left to right) *Francys, Mary Alice's friend Jessie Gerk, Jane, and Mary Alice. Aileen's brother, William, is in front wearing Idwal's RAF cap.*

beautiful girl I ever saw was there," Idwal said. "She was dressed all in black and cried so hard during the whole service I thought she'd surely die too." Mrs. Garl's ex-husband was one of Steinwedell's pallbearers.

Five people, each known to me in some way, had met tragedy in Tuscaloosa: Mrs. Garl, Mrs. Huffman, Carl Knauer, Lois Williamson, and now George Steinwedell. How sad that made me.

In June 1942, thirty-five white draftees left for induction into the armed forces. The Victory Committee provided a band, and a crowd of people was there to bid them farewell. A few days later one hundred more left. Then a set of Black draftees left, with the exuberant Industrial Band to see them off.

At forty-nine years old, Daddy had to register for the draft. We weren't worried about him having to go into the military; we knew his work on the railroad was too important to the war effort. Troop trains were constantly crisscrossing the country at Palos, Alabama, where he now at last had a regular job as third-trick operator. Sometimes he had as many as nine trains in a night.

During this time, business at Kress was very good. However, some customers, before buying any article, searched out the fine print to see where it was made. They thought they were striking a blow to Japan if they refused to buy anything that was labeled "Made in Japan" or "Made in Nippon." They didn't seem to realize that the money for the product had a long time back gone to Japan. The one who was hurt by their action was Kress, but I said nothing because I knew the public wanted to hurt the country that had hurt us so seriously.

At last I told Mr. Skelton I was leaving Kress. I had nothing definite in sight for the future but I didn't mention that. He stood silent, thumping one of the glass guards for the counters up and down, up and down. Without looking at me he said, "Whatever you do, don't go into nursing." He was from up north; his narrow view surprised me. But Brother-in-law Clarence too was outspoken about my decision. "Nurses are a bad lot," he said. "Worse than dime store floozies."

I well knew the quality of most of the Kress salesgirls. And many of our extra salesgirls were students at the University of Alabama during the week. If people were so mistaken about dime store workers, I reasoned, they could be mistaken about women in nursing.

But by now the focus of my attention had changed to the Women's Army Corps. As soon as Clarence heard that, he said, "When you get out of the WACs you'll be a ruined woman."

But Mama said, "I'd join myself if I were free."

———

Harry and I quit Kress the same night. He planned to join the army. Saying goodbye to Harry was hard for me. I so wanted to clasp his hand and tell him how much he meant to me and how I appreciated his help during my four years at work. But custom forbade it—I was a white woman, he was a Black man. We stood facing each other at the door where he had so often let me out at the end of a workday.

"Take care, Harry" was all I could say past the lump in my throat. "Take good care of yourself, hear?"

"You too, Miss Kilgore."

We gave each other a last look. I turned and went out. I heard the lock click behind me.

———

Even after leaving Kress, it took me a while to make the final decision to join the Women's Army Corps. I knew no woman who had ever considered joining the military. My weight was a stumbling block. The recruiting office told me I made the highest score on the IQ tests so far from our region but I was too much underweight. They had to wire somewhere to ask for special permission to accept me. When the answer yes came, I got myself ready, ruination or not.

Soon I was on the train to Fort Oglethorpe, Georgia, for basic training, along with many other future soldiers. In a few weeks' time most of these girls in frivolous dresses and flowered hats were transformed into serious women in plain uniforms. After basic training, I was sent to Ellington Field, Texas, a training station for navigators. Six of us new arrivals had mechanical aptitude and our company commander, a woman, wanted us to be assigned as airplane engine mechanics. The commandant of the field, a man, objected. "No women on the flight line," he said. Eventually our CO won, and we six became the first women assigned to work on the flight line in the Sixth Service Command. The male mechanics, mostly from California and Texas, were welcoming to us. They helped us in every way, but having women mechanics also gave them a convenient place to lay blame when something went wrong. The time an engine fell off a plane during the test run, an insistent cry went up: "The WACs did it! The WACs did it!" But when the work order was checked, not a single WAC's name was on it, much to our relief. The Californians never cussed in my hearing but they had an all-purpose exclamation that tickled me: "Rowdy Dow!"

Word came from McDade one more time. On his next furlough when he didn't find me at Kress, he went to see Jane at McLellan's. Her brief note on the back of her letter told me all I ever knew about his visit: "I almost forgot. McDade asked about you. When I told him you were working on airplane engines he said, 'I'd hate to fly in a plane she worked on.'"

I kept a diary of my new, sometimes bewildering life in the Women's Army Corps. My diary, published in 2001 as *Stateside Soldier*, shows that the lurid tales about the women who served in the military were as false as the tales told about "dime store floozies." I was not a ruined woman. Instead, after the war, I at long last realized my ambition to go to college, thanks to the GI Bill. I attended Judson College in Marion, Alabama, then studied writing and education at the University of Alabama, eventually getting a master's degree.

EPILOGUE

AT THIS WRITING I AM ninety-nine years old. I realize now that for much of my life, whatever I was doing, some people attempted to label me and place me in a group they could look down on. First, the ugliest child, then the humanized rat, followed by a dime store floozie and a woman soldier who was ridiculed on the street with chants of "wacky WAC quacky quack." I think that latter part of my life was the hardest but my previous experiences toughened me for it. From other soldiers I heard comments like "You're from Alabama? Poor thing!" and "Everybody knows Southern women are illiterate and immoral."

Most remarks like these I left behind when I was shipped out of basic training to Ellington Field. But when I went into Houston with several other enlisted women for our Saturday night treat of French onion soup at the Rice Hotel, crossing the lobby to the dining room was an obstacle course of officers shouting their room numbers at us, pressing their room keys on us, and in other ways acting like unruly school boys, not officers and gentlemen of the United States military. Staying on the post was the safest place from ridicule but even there animosity flared. As I hurried to work down the broad palm-lined main avenue of the post, a much-decorated combat returnee I'd never seen before spat on me.

But an enlisted man with whom I'd become good friends caught me off guard. I saw him one night come into the crowded lobby of the theater where I worked after hours. He was with a lieutenant. They stood a short distance away, but by focusing I could understand them above the noise of the exuberant GIs waiting for the movie to begin.

"There she is," my friend said proudly, nodding toward me. Out of the corner of my eye I saw the lieutenant look me over from head to foot.

Distinctly he said, "Man, you can do better than that!"

Whether my friend took the officer's evaluation or not, I was careful to stay out of his way after that to avoid unpleasant reminders.

Unfortunately, a teeny tiny seed of hope in my heart refused to die. Working on the flight line one blue-gold afternoon in warm sun and cool breezes from the Gulf, Marge Perkins and I were perched with our toolboxes on the wing of an advanced trainer. Both of us were corporals and both of us wore our HBT coveralls with a GI cap (all in a distinctive herring-bone-twill). Thrilled with the day, thrilled with the world, I stood up and proclaimed, as I looked over the airfield at the parked aircraft of every description, "So fair and foul a day I have not seen."

"Shakespeare," Perkins said. "Macbeth."

That started us on quotations and poems while we worked; she had a whole library of them stored in her memory. And besides being smart and beautiful, she was savvy about fashions, plays, and the movie world. She could sit for hours cross-legged on her bed studying Houston and Dallas newspapers, especially the department store ads and the social sections.

Now in a frenzy of joy, I said something off the cuff, what I can't now recall because the next thing that happened wiped it out of my mind. Anyway, Perkins laughed heartily at whatever it was. She said, as she tampered with a screw, "I swanee, Kilgore, you are absolutely the most fantastic, cutest person in this whole wide world . . ." She paused to adjust her screwdriver while my heart soared. Perkins, the sophisticate, the glamour-savvy cover girl, recognizes that I am beautiful, because "cute" is another word for "beauty," or at least "pretty." How wrong everybody has been about me, people just wouldn't see me, when here Marge Perkins of Lufkin, Texas, recognizes me with true eyes . . . She laid down the screwdriver and continued, ". . . to be so ugly."

My heart could hardly sustain the plunge from the heights of my thoughts down to the depths of my growing-up days. Wildly, I looked around. The sun was extinguished, the sky was indigo, I felt alone on the wing of a plane in Texas. I turned away to hide my face.

Just then the Catholic chaplain stopped by, young and smiling. While he and Perkins chatted, I quietly closed my toolbox. With it in hand, I fumbled my way down to the tarmac and crept back into the hangar to a secret place behind the tool shanty. There, heaped in a corner, I washed my face ten times over in all the tears I had refused to shed, from Uncle Pat to Perkins, crying, crying more, crying some more.

I had cared. Of course I had cared. And I cared now, deeply. But in the past, to save myself, I could never acknowledge that I cared. Even so the wounds, still there, would not go away. What to do? How to rid myself of the years of hurt? In that little room of despair, I faced the truth: to be healed, I had to accept and forgive. This was the one way to free myself. Accept. Forgive. Forget. Hard words. Impossible words. "But I will do it," I vowed. "With God's help, I will do it. I will accept myself as I am and I will accept those who object to me as I am. And I will hold no grudges."

Finally, with the sure knowledge that what I aimed for was possible, I stood in the dark, straightened my shoulders, smoothed my hair, and put on my HBT cap. With my hand on the doorknob, I took a deep breath before coming out from that dark nook into an even darker hangar. Everybody had gone except for Price, a WAC who sat at the entrance with fountain pen and a pile of papers. We spoke as I passed on my way to the WAC area for mess and night detail.

I did leave the past behind me, back of that tool shanty, in the secret place. It wasn't easy by any means but I came out free, thank God.

After the war, people sometimes looked askance at me because I had been in the army. At the college I attended, my freshman year I was domiciled in a townie's house. No room for me in the school dormitories, the housing staff explained. But I later learned there'd been plenty of space; they'd feared I'd be a bad influence on the other students with my worldly experience. When I transferred to the University of Alabama, one fraternity somehow found out that I was a veteran. Often I could not avoid walking past that fraternity. Every time, someone there saw me and alerted others and they all sent up a

*The Kilgore sisters at the end of World War II in
1945: (front row, left to right) Mary Alice and
Aileen in WAC uniforms, (back row, left to right)
Francys and Jane.*

chant familiar to me from the war years: "Wacky, wacky, quacky, WAC,
quack, quack!"

Once I earned my bachelor of science degree, I taught school, but
that did not elevate me in the public's respect. A saying common in
Tuscaloosa County disheartened me more than most anything else:
"Those who can, do. Those who can't, teach." In addition, a teacher's
pay was barely enough to live on, and class size was high (forty-two
fourth graders!). Yet my students were wonderful to work with, and
their parents, ranging from professional people to sharecroppers,
were supportive. One of my students turned out to be the son of Mrs.
Faucett, the high school teacher who had encouraged me to become a
writer.

No matter what label was pinned on me, life was always filled with
new things to learn, with much beauty and humor. My attitude was
due mostly to my upbringing, to the ideals of Daddy and Mama, and
to the wonderful people I met along the way—my teachers, customers

and fellow workers in the dime store, military personnel at Ellington Field, my students and their parents.

Eventually I realized my earliest ambition, that of creating stories, as Aunt Mittie did, and becoming a published writer. My first book came out from Milkweed Editions of Minneapolis when I was seventy-four years old. *The Summer of the Bonepile Monster* won two awards: the Milkweed Prize for Children's Literature and the Alabama Library Association Award. One reviewer put into words my writing aim: "This story makes reality an enchantment." I had learned the hard way that reality can be an enchantment, but we must work to make it so.